# MOU
# BIKE GUIDE

## Mountain Bike Guide
## North York Moors

**by**

# Sarah & Gary McLeod

NATIONAL PARK
BOUNDARY

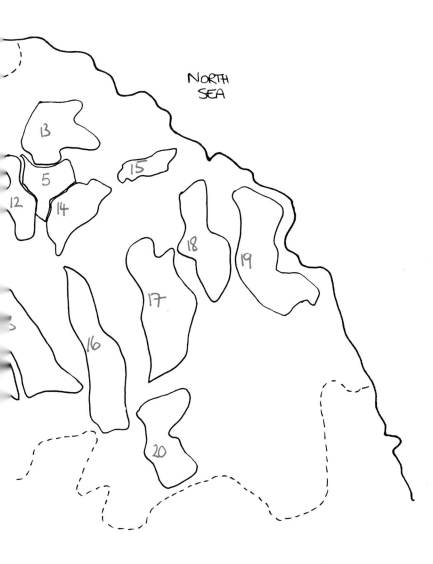

NORTH
SEA

13

15

5

12

14

18

19

17

16

20

## Acknowledgements:

We would like to express sincere thanks to the following, whose assistance has been invaluable in the compilation of this guide;

North York Moors National Park Authority rights of way officers, Helmsley.

North Yorkshire County Council Highways Department, Northallerton.

North Yorkshire County Council Archives Department, Northallerton, for location of public domain mapping reference sources.

Scarborough Borough Council rights of way officer, Pickering.

Traveleads and Evans of Leeds plc for computer facilities.

Alan Hope and Bob Orr for use of camera equipment.

Mike Shepherdson and Ian Millar for accompanying on route-checking rides.

The Forestry Commission, Pickering, for access permission over their lands in route 20.

The publishers acknowledge editorial and production supervision by Susan Hodgkiss.

# CONTENTS

## Introduction

In terms of landscape, the North York Moors owe their present aspect to the Ice Age, when the effects of glaciation carved out the deep valleys and smoothed off the high moor tops to create the basic topography of the moors.

The glacial actions left exposed or accessible a wide variety of geological strata which over the centuries have influenced the usage of the moors by its inhabitants: from the earliest Iron Age settlers and the Roman military and civilian immigrants; through the time of the harrying by the Norse invaders; on to the period of expansion by the monastic orders; right through to the time of the Victorian industrialists and their exploitation of the mineral resources of the moors. The area has also witnessed the latest practices of agriculture and industry, many of which have left clear reminders of times past in the new predominantly agricultural area.

The moors today still have widely varied uses – from the potash mine on the coast near Loftus, to the moors managed for grouse shooting and sheep grazing – but the industrial usage has greatly declined in favour of agriculture and the newest industry, tourism, which is where this guide comes in.

The moors offer a tremendously wide variety of attractions to naturalists, walkers, geologists, sportsmen and, in recent years, mountain bikers. Well aware of the concerns voiced by landowners, National Park Authorities, walkers and other users about mountain bikers using the moors, we decided to work out a number of circular routes which would allow mountain bikers to enjoy a range of rides around the moors, yet stay on legitimate bridleways and public highways – thus avoiding conflicts with landowners and others. For this reason we stress that the guide be used in conjunction with the Ordnance Survey maps, in order to ensure that you stay on the correct route.

Although the majority of bikers will be summer visitors to the moors, there will be hardier people who will decide to visit the moors during the autumn, winter and spring months. For these visitors, the safety and survival notes are particularly designed to ensure that due consideration is given to your own safety, and that of others.

Whenever you visit the North York Moors you are guaranteed spectacular scenery, interesting rides and good pubs, hotels and restaurants – so take the time to explore, whether visiting from further afield or living in the area – use this guide as a basis for working out your own routes from the OS maps and discover the fun in route finding.

## Orientation

Map references in this book relate to the Ordnance Survey Outdoor Leisure Series of maps – North York Moors Western Area (map 26) and North York Moors Eastern Area (map 27) published on the scale of 1:25 000 (2.5 inches to 1 mile).

You should NOT attempt to follow ANY of these rides without the aid of the relevant OS map and a compass. Whilst the route descriptions and sketch maps are easily followed in good weather, you must be able to locate and follow alternative routes should conditions dictate, and a map and compass will enable you to locate and reach the nearest surfaced roads and shelter in the shortest amount of time.

Map references firstly give EASTINGS – the grid lines running from north to south on your map, then NORTHINGS – the grid lines running from west to east on the map.

Example:

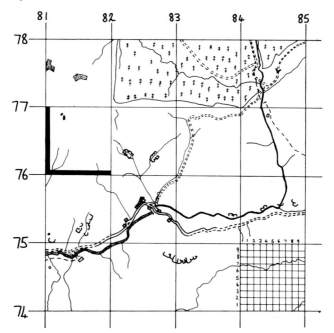

## Rights of way

The description of any route in this document does not guarantee that a right of way exists. Whilst checks have been undertaken with the various authorities concerned to ensure that the majority of routes are on public bridleways, public highways, byways open to all traffic and unsurfaced tracks linking public highways, changes in designation on some routes may affect access to some areas described in this publication. If in doubt, check with Local Authority and National Park offices for up-to-date and definitive maps showing public access.

**Route descriptions**
Route descriptions include total mileage, split into on road/off road distances, and an estimate of the time it should take an averagely fit person to cycle the route, allowing for brief stops on the way, or meal breaks on longer routes.

There are no gradings given to the individual routes, as all areas of the moors should be equally accessible to most off road riders. Most rides include some walking or carrying of cycles, but none require serious climbing or take you into any particularly hazardous areas; however care should be taken at all times, and there are notes on safety further on in the book.

When considering the suitability of a route, do take time to study your OS map and understand the contour 'picture' of the ride, i.e. the amount of climbing and descending. In deciding the routes, we attempted to structure them with a minimum amount of severe climbing and a maximum number of descents.

**Definition of the "Get Off And Walk" (GOAW) factor:**
This will be shown as a number corresponding to the approximate accumulated number of miles on the route over which a normally fit person on a standard bike would probably get off and walk – rather than flog themselves to death for the sake of appearances or pure personal pride. The reason for walking is normally a severe gradient, but occasionally it may be down to a very poor surface or a

dangerous section. These rides are about having fun, taking the time to look at and appreciate some extraordinary countryside, sampling some very good pubs and enjoying yourself with friends – they are not about posing in front of other riders or training for the Iron Man event. So do not be afraid of taking a breather whenever you feel the need – and ride to your own limits, not those of other people or what you think you should be capable of – greater stamina will develop only with time and regular exercise.

**Safety and emergency procedures**
Whilst the valleys of The North York Moors are fairly well inhabited, and the area as a whole is within easy reach for many people, you should not forget that there are very large areas of open moorland, and weather conditions can alter very rapidly – even on a summer's day. Should you have an accident or become lost or stranded in bad weather, you need to know the basics about looking after yourself or a companion, as well as knowing how to help others who may be searching for you.

The minimalist approach of 'racing' mountain bikers is not relevant if you are going to equip yourself for longer distance riding and route finding, and the following should be viewed as essential items to keep you moving and to cope with emergencies;

Helmet – there are plenty of rocks to land on, so wear one!

Tool kit – to include pump, tyre levers, spare tube, tube repair kit, multi-purpose tool (eg Cool Tool). Everything you need will fit into an expander saddle bag.

Map and compass – an orienteer's map case keeps maps dry and easy to read.

A bike computer is an optional, but *very* handy, item. They are pretty widely available at reasonable prices nowadays and increase the accuracy of your route-finding wonderfully.

Whistle and micro torch. (Fit into map case).

Space type survival blanket/bag (folds smaller than a bar of chocolate, so storage no problem).

First-aid kit – Extra layer of waterproof/warm clothing and some type of emergency food/drink. (Probably best stored in a pannier system or rucksack – depends on personal preference).

It is also not a good idea to cycle alone on the moors – in case of an accident which requires someone to ride for assistance – and in case of any doubts on route finding, when two heads are always better than one. Leave details of your route with someone at home and let them know what time you expect to start and finish – not forgetting to let them know if you deliberately delay your return home, so as not to spark off a full-scale rescue unnecessarily.

There are mountain rescue teams around the moors, and these will be called upon by the emergency services (usually the police) if necessary, so 999 is the only number you need to know if seeking help for an injured rider. If you are injured yourself, or are leaving an injured and conscious rider, try to remember the simple rules below:

In poor weather conditions, keep yourself/them warm – use extra clothing and survival blankets straight away and do not allow heat to be lost first. Insulate casualty from cold ground and check for injuries. Shooting butts abound on the moors – and are marked on the OS maps – and they are often ideal shelters from the wind, as are the leeward sides of dry-stone walls. Heather is a good insulator and even a dry ditch or hollow can assist in staying out of a chilling wind or driving rain.

11

First-aid may need to be administered prior to seeking help, and it is important that everyone venturing on to the moors has a basic knowledge of the subject, and how to assist an unconscious or conscious casualty. We do not propose to write details of first-aid practices, not being qualified to do so, but would recommend riders to attend one of the short courses run by the St. John's Ambulance Association or the British Red Cross Society. You should also obtain, read and keep with you the booklet 'Safety in the Mountains', published by the British Mountaineering Council, which gives valuable advice on emergency procedures. The British Mountaineering Council can be contacted on 061 273 5835.

Whistle/torch can be used to attract help or to assist searchers pinpoint a person. Six blasts on the whistle, or six flashes on the torch, repeated after 1 minute intervals, are the recognised distress signals in mountain rescue situations.

If there are more than two riders, one person should stay with the injured person while one goes for help. If there are more than three, then two should go for help. Remember – if going for help, do not take risks that could jeopardise your safety and lead to injury to yourself – this could turn a controlled situation into a real emergency. If there are only two riders, mark the location of the injured person with some white or bright clothing or item, to assist location of the casualty when rescuers arrive.

Take a detailed note/description of the location of the injured person, and full details of their injuries and condition when left. Note the time of the accident and when you left the casualty.

If any of the above recommendations seem to be over-cautious, just have a good look around when you are on top of one of the high moors, and then imagine yourself injured or with an injured companion, daylight fading, temperatures dropping and maybe rain or snow falling. You might then consider that safety cannot be ignored on the principle that 'it'll never happen to me', especially in a sport like mountain biking where the terrain and physical nature of the activity are a recipe for falls and equipment damage which need to be coped with competently.

## Clothing

It is a good idea to adopt the layer approach to clothing – basically wearing several layers of thin clothing which can be varied to suit conditions, protected overall by something windproof and waterproof. A change of clothes at the end of your ride is also sensible, as you are likely to arrive back wet and dirty.

As we have said before, helmets should be viewed as essential, as almost every ride we do could involve some falling off – usually in holes hidden in puddles or as a result of hitting rocks at the wrong angle. Gloves help protect hands during falls and help keep backs of hands warm on cold days.

Footwear should have a sole with good grip, and in winter should be waterproof. Wet feet are not so bad in summer, but in winter can be a severe liability and dangerous.

Try always in winter to think about keeping extremities warm and dry. A balaclava under your helmet is great for your ears and face. If you can avoid having to think about how cold you are, you will enjoy the ride much more and have the concentration required to ride safely.

## The bike

Your bike is a matter of personal choice and budget – but as long as it is well-maintained and has adequate tyres, most bikes will cope with all of the routes in this book. (Your own fitness is more of a question in determining which ride to undertake!) Make sure you have enough basic equipment to keep the bike moving – spare tube, combination spanner, allen keys, tyre levers, pump and tube repair kit. A rack on your bike is a great way to avoid a back soaked with perspiration from carrying a rucksack, and acts as a sort of rear mudguard.

## Environment – Use of the moors by mountain bikers

Although a large part of the moors may look open and desolate, there are a lot of people using them, and a lot of people making their living from them. It is therefore in everyone's interest that mountain bikers have a positive attitude towards the safeguarding of the moors and that they co-operate with landowners, farmers and National Park authorities to ensure they do not cause any damage when riding. The most basic rules are spelled out in the Country Code and the Off Road Code, as follows;

**The Country Code** – issued by The Countryside Commission. (Brackets are author's own comments)

Enjoy the countryside and respect its life and work.
Guard against all risk of fire. (Vitally important on heather moors!)
Fasten all gates.
Keep your dogs under close control. (If biking, do not take dogs.)

Keep to public paths across farmland. (Bridleways for bikers)
Use gates and stiles to cross fences, hedges and walls.
Leave livestock, crops and machinery alone.
Take your litter home.
Help keep all water clean.
Protect wildlife, plants and trees.
Take special care on country roads.
Make no unnecessary noise.

**The Off Road Code** – Issued by the Mountain Bike Club

Only ride where you know you have a legal right.
Always yield to horses and pedestrians.
Avoid animals and crops. In some circumstances this may not
be possible, at which times contact should be kept to a
minimum.
Take all litter with you.
Leave all gates as found.
Keep the noise down.
Don't get annoyed with anyone, it never solves any problems.
Always try to be self-sufficient, for you and your bike.
Never create a fire hazard.

   Although the routes in this guide are principally based on
bridleways, tracks and roads believed to be rights of way, you
should never forget that you are nearly always on someone's
land, and should show due respect in any situation where
your right of access is called into question. Be polite and ask
for clarification with regard to your position on the map and
point out if your map shows you to have a right of way. If
denied access for whatever reason, do not resort to argument
– this only worsens the situation for you, and possibly other

bikers after you – but leave the area and take the question of access up with the local authorities. At certain times of year, such as the lambing season, grouse hatching season or shooting days – it is wise to consider leaving out a route that is likely to conflict with these activities. At all times of year be considerate of the wildlife and livestock on the moors.

**Preventing erosion of tracks**
Many of the moorland tracks suffer from erosion as a result of walkers avoiding wet and muddy areas, and thus spreading the area of the track sideways. Mountain bikers should be very conscious of the effect of off road tyres on wetter tracks, and ensure that they always stick to the centre of tracks, regardless of getting a bit wet – which is, after all, part of the fun. By keeping this principle in mind, you will never be accused of causing damage to the trails you are using, and landowners inspecting tracks will not have cause to dispute biker's access to tracks on their property. Try to fit the widest section tyres that your bike will permit, to further moderate any damage you may cause.

**Forestry Commission areas**
We have been asked by the Forestry Commission to point out the dangers of riding in the vicinity of timber harvesting equipment, as the operatives of such equipment will be unable to hear you approaching due to noise levels. Please take extra care in such areas and keep clear of lorries, tractors etc.

## KEY TO MAPS

SURFACED ROAD

OFF ROAD SECTION

WOODED AREA

RAILWAY LINE

RIVER OR STREAM

TRIG POINT

BUILDINGS

T. TELEPHONE BOX

FOOTPATH

17

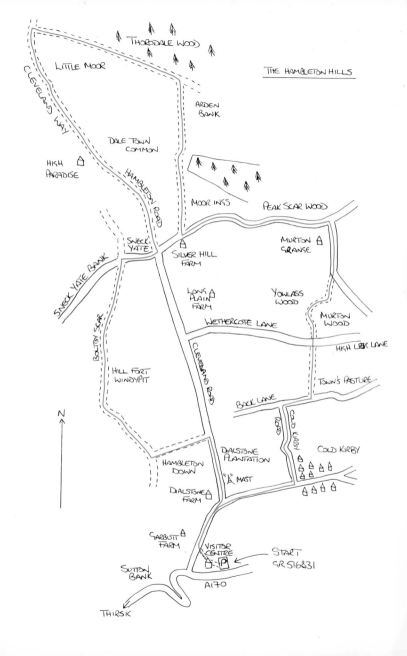

# WESTERN AREA

## 1. THE HAMBLETON HILLS

Map          – OS 26

Start point  – GR516831 – Carpark at the top of Sutton Bank, next to the Visitor Centre.

Distance     – 16.5 miles (11.5 miles off road/5 miles on road).

Time         – approximately 3.5 hours.

GOAW factor – 1.

**Introduction:**
This route follows the line of cliffs running from Whitestone Cliff, above Gormire Lake, northwards to Sneck Yate Bank. It offers tremendous views over the northern Vale of York and across towards The Dales. It can be a very strenuous ride in muddy conditions and care needs to be taken on the cliff top section as the bridleway veers close to the cliff edge in places. Due to the popularity of this area with walkers (many of whom are the Sunday after-lunch variety) we suggest that this ride is best undertaken on a weekday, and probably best left until a dry spell occurs.

**The route:**

From the carpark, take the minor road north towards Dial-stone Farm. Turn left immediately before the farm, onto a bridleway heading left, south-west, towards Whitestone Cliff. Follow the bridleway for 0.5 miles and you will get onto the clifftop bridleway over a stile in the corner of the field (please use the stile to ensure that no further damage is done to the dry-stone wall which has already suffered some abuse). Turn right on the new bridleway and follow it north as it meanders its way along the clifftop. You pass by a few disused quarries and your bridleway is joined by several others from both west and east. You continue in your northerly direction for around 1.5 miles until you arrive at Sneck Yate, where Sneck Yate Bank crosses your bridleway diagonally west to east.

Turn right onto the road and climb uphill. Follow the road for a couple of hundred yards until you see the sign on your left-hand side for the Forestry Commission lands in Boltby. Turn left at the junction and you are on the Hambleton Road. This road leads you roughly north-west for about 0.75 miles where it is joined by the Cleveland Way just above High Paradise Farm. It then continues north-west, passing by the eastern edge of some woods and Steeple Cross. After another 1.5 miles, you meet another bridleway on the left and as the two join, you swing due north over Little Moor.

At the point where the road up from Kepwick Quarry crosses your route (identified by the "no access to traffic" signs), turn right and ride south-east towards Arden Bank. Ride across the moor and go through two gates (leaving them as you find them). After approx. 1.5 miles you reach the treeline on your left where you will see a very distinct track turning right and climbing up into the field above you. Follow this track and travel due south, heading for the extreme

Gormire Lake from Sutton Bank *Photo: Paul Hannon*

western end of the woods which can be seen ahead to your left. Ignore the left turning just before the woods and continue straight on past the woods. Go straight on again at the next bridleway crossroads and continue straight ahead towards Silver Hill Farm. Here you turn left onto Peak Scar Road.

Follow this road past the Peak Scar climbing area, identified by the green signs on the fence to your left. Just beyond that point you come to a T-junction where you turn right. Pass Murton Grange on your right and head south again. Shortly after leaving the buildings your road forks and you continue heading roughly south on a bridleway towards the disused quarry at Murton Wood. On reaching the quarry, there is a steep descent, marked by bridleway signs, to the floor of the valley. The bridleway crosses the footbridge over Limperdale Gill before commencing the steep push up the other side (fortunately there is a bench halfway up!).

At the top of the climb, head in a straight line along the edge of the field to the road. Cross the road to the right and then after 10 yards turn left to pick up the bridleway again. Follow this until you reach Back Lane, above Cold Kirby. Turn right onto Back Lane and then left along Cold Kirby Road just as far as the T-junction at Chapel Cottage. Here you turn right and stay on this road back to the carpark, passing the Dialstone Farm junction on your way.

National Park sign. *Photo: Paul Hannon*

Hawnby Hill from the south. *Photo: Paul Hannon*

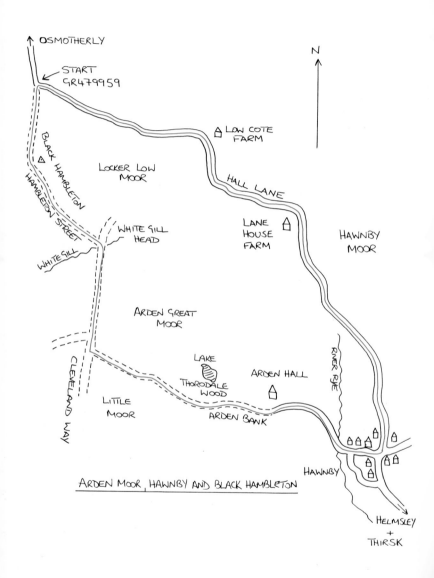

OSMOTHERLY

START
GR479959

N

LOW COTE
FARM

BLACK HAMBLETON

HAMBLETON STREET

LOCKER LOW
MOOR

HALL LANE

WHITE GILL
HEAD

WHITEGILL

LANE
HOUSE
FARM

HAWNBY
MOOR

ARDEN GREAT
MOOR

CLEVELAND WAY

LAKE

THORODALE
WOOD

ARDEN HALL

RIVER RYE

LITTLE
MOOR

ARDEN BANK

HAWNBY

HELMSLEY
+
THIRSK

ARDEN MOOR, HAWNBY AND BLACK HAMBLETON

## 2.  ARDEN MOOR, HAWNBY AND BLACK HAMBLETON

Map          – OS 26

Start point  – GR479959 – Unmarked carpark under Black
               Hambleton on the Osmotherley – Hawnby
               road.

Distance     – Total 13.5 miles (5.5 miles off road/8 miles on
               road).

Time         – Approximately 2 – 2.5 hours.

GOAW factor – 2

**Introduction:**
This route takes in some of the gentler landscape along the
western edge of the moors, and is a good ride for people who
do not have lots of confidence with map reading as you really
cannot go wrong on this ride. It also has the handily-located
Hawnby Hotel about half way along the route – so if you are
new to mountain biking you can perhaps pause for a breather
and some liquid encouragement before tackling the off road
section of the ride. The ascent up to the old drover's road is
fairly well-surfaced and the grass climb onto Black
Hambleton is very easy going, followed by a long enough
descent to whet anyone's appetite for more dramatic stuff.

This ride is split fifty-fifty between on road and off road,
with the first part covering the fairly quiet road between

Osmotherley and Hawnby. Little description of the first 8 miles is necessary, as there is only the one metalled road to follow from setting off from the carpark until you reach Hawnby, at the head of Rye Dale. The road does include some steep climbs and descents in the first 5 miles, but the final approach to Hawnby is easy going.

**The route:**
Leave the carpark travelling south-east towards Hawnby. You follow this road, passing by some woods. There is an enjoyable descent to Low Cote Farm after which you begin to climb again along Hall Lane. A pleasant descent from Lane House Farm takes you through Ellers Wood. From there you continue travelling south on a relatively easy road until you reach Hawnby, approx. 5.5 miles from the start point.

When you arrive in Hawnby, follow the road as it turns right into the village, and immediately carry straight on where the main road turns sharp left after only another few yards. If you are ready for a break, you will pass the Hawnby Hotel on your left, if not, carry on towards Arden Hall. On reaching the hall, you continue travelling west. The metalled road ends here and continues on a track through Thorodale Wood. On leaving the shelter of Thorodale Wood, you will come out onto the exposed moor. You now begin the climb up on to the old drover's road – Hambleton Street, now a section of the Cleveland Way running northwards across Arden Great Moor. Follow the unfenced track to arrive on Hambleton Street, opposite the gate leading down through the disused Kepwick Quarry.

Turn right here, and follow the broad path of the Cleveland Way which runs due north until White Gill Head. Here it turns sharp left and climbs along the western flank of Black

The bottom of the descent from Black Hambleton

Hambleton. From the high point of the track, above the wooded slopes of Nether Silton Moor, you can have some fun on the descent down Hambleton End – being careful of some of the deeper ruts which are encountered when you have built up speed towards the lower part of the descent. The end of the route is clearly visible as you ride down the hill, passing through some gates on the way (closing them after you). The carpark will be reached shortly thereafter.

# CARLTON MOOR AND SCUSDALE

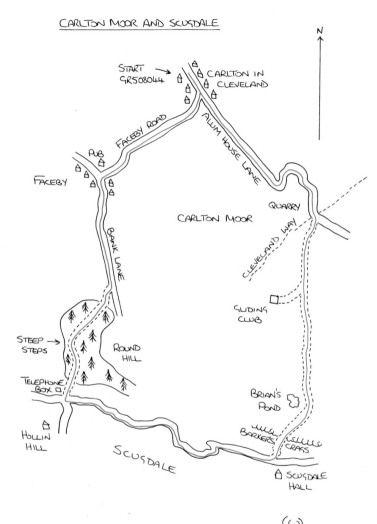

N

START
GR508044

CARLTON IN
CLEVELAND

FACEBY ROAD

ALUM HOUSE LANE

PUB

FACEBY

QUARRY

CARLTON MOOR

CLEVELAND WAY

BANK LANE

GLIDING
CLUB

STEEP
STEPS

ROUND
HILL

TELEPHONE
BOX

BRIAN'S
POND

HOLLIN
HILL

BARKERS
CRAGS

SCUSDALE

SCUSDALE
HALL

BILSDALE MAST
(ON HORIZON)

## 3. CARLTON MOOR AND SCUGDALE

Map — OS 26

Start point — GR508044 — The village of Carlton in Cleveland.

Distance — 7.5 miles (3 miles off road/4.5 miles on road).

Time — Approximately 2 hours.

GOAW factor — 2

**Introduction:**
This is a quiet ride, although there are quite a few roads involved. It has only one serious climb at the beginning, when your legs should be up to it. The area where the Cleveland Way crosses your route is pretty popular with hang-gliders and on a bright, breezy weekend the air seems full of them, added to by the presence of the gliding club further up around the hillside. This might give you a clue as to the weather conditions in this area – it is probably a route best done on a warmer day so that you do not suffer from wind chill quite so much. Navigation is easy and there is an excellent pub in Faceby for those who feel the need to reward themselves at the end of the ride.

**The route:**
From the village, head due south-east towards the moors along Alum House Lane – signposted to Chop Gate. The lane follows the edge of Busby Wood for a short while. After leaving the wood you begin the very long climb up through the disused quarries to the top of Carlton Bank. At the top of the bank you will see The Cleveland Way signposted directly ahead of you. Go through a gate and onto the bridleway leading to the eastern side of the summit of Carlton Moor. Stay to the right-hand track when it forks not long after the beginning of the bridleway. This will lead you due south to the gliding club on the moor top.

When reaching the gliding club, take the bridleway to your left heading directly towards the easily seen Bilsdale transmitter mast. (If there is low cloud this is the wide bridleway due south). This takes you over Bilsdale West Moor for under 1 mile directly towards Brian's Pond. Here you will see a bridleway sign pointing you to the right immediately after the pond. The bridleway becomes very indistinct, but after a few hundred yards you will reach the rocky outcrop of Barker's Crags – take care not to ride too close to the edge. Head to the left and you will find a path down through the rocks. This leads to a gateway on your left which allows you to descend the hillside directly towards Scugdale Hall and the road heading west along Scugdale.

Turn right onto the road and follow it mainly due west for around 2 miles until you reach a telephone box at the junction above Hollin Hill. Here you will see the Cleveland Way signposted to your right heading up into the woodland of Live Moor Plantation. Follow this track around the hillside and climb up the very steep steps to Knolls End. At the top of the steps, take the track to your left and descend through the

At the top of Carlton Bank

woods. Go straight ahead through the gate in front of you when the track turns sharply back on itself.

At the other end of the woods, cross the corner of the field (watch out for the drop going through the gate) and turn left onto Bank Lane. Follow this lane with Whorl Hill Wood on your left to the village of Faceby. In the village, turn right at the Sutton Arms and follow the road back into Carlton in Cleveland, another mile or so further on.

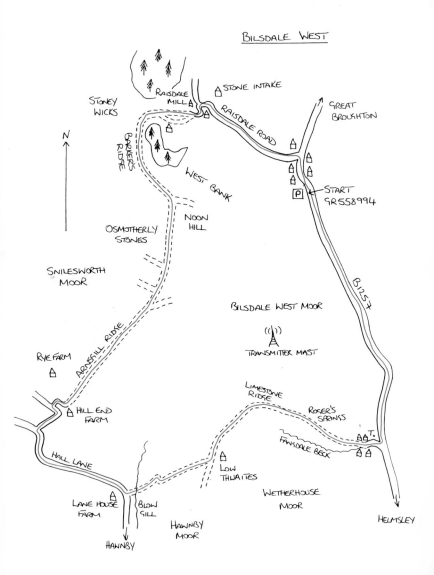

BILSDALE WEST

## 4. BILSDALE WEST

Map           – OS 26

Start point   – GR558994 Carpark at Chop Gate village hall.

Distance      – 16 miles (11 miles off road/5 miles on road).

Time          – Approximately 4 – 5 hours.

GOAW factor – 2.

**Introduction:**
Very open, sometimes desolate terrain dominates this ride, but with fair or good weather conditions it is a superb ride which gives you a feeling of great space around you. Probably not a route for very poor weather conditions as there is little shelter and not enough close-in interest if you have to keep your head down in the wind and rain – this is a "big country" type ride and a blue sky makes all the difference. Navigation is difficult in places but the going is only moderately strenuous, so take time to look around and link the terrain to your map and route description, and you should not go far wrong.

**The route:**
From the carpark, turn left and ride north through the village of Chop Gate. Take the first turning on the left onto Raisdale Road and head north-east until you reach Raisdale Mill. At the mill, turn in and go between the buildings on your left. Then turn right uphill to the beginning of the climb up Mill Lane.

At this stage, look out for a marker post with a blue arrow on your right, which signifies the commencement of the green lane which climbs in the direction of Stoney Wicks. Keep to this track, which takes you to the right of the farm and yard at the top of Mill Lane – the track through the farmyard is designated as a footpath only and is also a play area for children. You will probably have to walk up the green lane until past the farm. When you emerge from the deeper cut part of the lane onto the more open moor, you will see the bridleway turning around to your left above the tree line and heading in the direction of the Bilsdale transmitter mast.

Climb up along Barker's Ridge directly towards the mast. As the track levels out you will notice another track forking to the left – ignore this, it is a footpath. Continue south, descending now. After about 0.5 miles of descent, you will pass another track on the left, and then begin to descend in a south-westerly direction along Arnsgill Ridge on Snilesworth Moor. This track gently descends the flank of Arnsgill Ridge, leading after about 1 mile to Hill End Farm. As you descend through a gate and along a lane into the farmyard, turn right – away from the farmhouse, and down the concrete track to Low Cote Farm and the Osmotherley to Hawnby Road.

Turn left here and follow the road for around a mile along Hall Lane until you reach Lane House Farm. Here you will see a bridleway marker on your left at a new gateway. Go through the gate and through the first field in a straight line. Then cross diagonally left across the second field, heading for the bottom left-hand corner of the second field and Blow Gill (assuming the fields are still grazing pasture only – if sown with crops please stick to the edges).

Cross the stream – you will have to wade it – and climb up the hillside opposite. To the left you will see a dry-stone wall

Looking over Blow Gill Beck from Lane House Farm

The Buck Inn, Chop Gate. *Photo: Paul Hannon*

also climbing the hill, and the Bilsdale transmitter mast again in front of you. The bridleway is totally indistinct at this point but you should veer right away from the wall and head approximately 10 degrees to the right of the mast, heading east-north-east uphill towards the high point of the moor. As you ascend the hill you will see some trees ahead on the skyline. Head for the right-hand ones which are just in front of Low Thwaites farm.

From Low Thwaites Farm, turn left – due north directly towards the mast again and follow the track until the end of the dry-stone wall on your right. At this point there is a track heading off to your right which can be followed for a short while. Then you need to break away left on the bridleway across the unmarked moor to descend Limestone Ridge directly towards Roger's Springs. If you stay on the track instead of breaking away you will find yourself on the wrong side of the Fangdale Beck valley and will need to descend, cross the beck, and climb up the other side to reach Roger's Springs.

At the end of Limestone Ridge you will see an indent which leads you towards a steep descent down the hill into Fangdale Beck. This part of the route is easy to follow but some care should be taken on the steeper parts of the descent. The fun is soon over as you arrive in Fangdale Beck. Follow a short stretch of seemingly unused lane between some cottages then turn left and cycle through the village. When you reach the main road (B1257) you turn left. The road runs north, following the River Seph and you follow it for some 3 miles to arrive back at Chop Gate and the start point.

Bridleway junction before descent into Fryup Dale

Bridleway stone and causeway. *Photo: Paul Hannon*

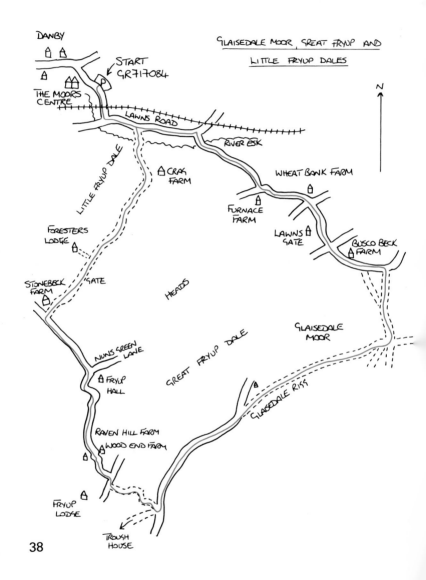

DANBY

START
GR 717084

THE MOORS
CENTRE

LAWNS ROAD

GLAISEDALE MOOR, GREAT FRYUP AND

LITTLE FRYUP DALES

N

RIVER ESK

LITTLE FRYUP DALE

CRAG
FARM

WHEAT BANK FARM

FORESTERS
LODGE

FURNACE
FARM

LAWNS
GATE

BUSCO BECK
FARM

STONEBECK
FARM

GATE

HEADS

GLAISEDALE
MOOR

GREAT FRYUP DALE

NUNS GREEN
LANE

FRYUP
HALL

GLAISEDALE RIGG

RAVEN HILL FARM

WOOD END FARM

FRYUP
LODGE

TROUSH
HOUSE

38

## 5. GLAISDALE MOOR, GREAT FRYUP AND LITTLE FRYUP DALES

Map         – OS 27

Start point  – GR717084 Carpark of The Moors Centre at Danby

Distance    – Total 9.4 miles (3.5 off road/6.9 on road)

Time       – Approximately 2 – 2.5 hours

GOAW factor – 1

**Introduction:**
This is a fairly easy ride which takes in the excellent views down both Fryup Dales from the River Esk, and then climbs up onto Glaisdale Rigg before crossing both of the Fryup Dales on the way back to Danby. No really hard off-road work is required, and the navigation is fairly easy. The route can be a muddy one, so a dry day will improve your enjoyment of the off-road section, especially when riding along Little Fryup Dale.

**The route:**
From the carpark at Danby, turn left and ride under the railway bridge, turning left shortly after, to follow Lawns

Road. After 1.4 miles you will reach a junction, signposted 'Fryup', where you need to turn right. Follow this road until you reach the T-junction at Furnace Farm, turn left and go straight ahead at the crossroads near Wheat Bank Farm and straight ahead again at the next crossroads, just after Lawns Gate. Past Busco Beck Farm you will see first one bridleway sign on your right, then, shortly after, another sign near a dry-stone wall and with a much more defined track than the first bridleway. You will now have completed 3.5 miles from your starting point.

Turn right, onto the bridleway, and ride due south uphill until you reach the top of the incline, begin to descend, and join the very distinct county road along Glaisdale Rigg which crosses your bridleway at right angles. Turn right onto the track and follow this south-west, climbing gently for just over another mile, until you join the road just south of the trig point on the top of Glaisdale Rigg.

Continue in the same direction along the road for 1 mile until you see a signpost to 'Trough House' and a bridleway sign which points 90 degrees towards north from the direction of the 'Trough House' sign. Leave the road and follow the direction of the small bridleway sign, crossing the poorly defined track across the moor for a few hundred yards until you arrive at the steep descent above Fryup Lodge, visible below you, to your left. The track down the hillside is pretty much a matter of guesswork, but you will clearly identify a double-walled lane at the foot of the hill, to the right of Fryup Lodge, and leading from the hillside to the lane linking the lodge and the road around Fryup Dale.

Join the lane from the lodge, and turn left when you join the road proper, in the direction of Wood End Farm. Follow the road for around another 1.3 miles until passing one

Looking south from Stump Cross on Slape Wath Moor

Danby Lodge. *Photo: Paul Hannon*

bridleway sign on your right, you arrive at Stonebeck Gate Farm. The bridleway sign at the farm is missing, but the bridleway runs straight past the front garden of the farmhouse and down the easily identified lane heading north-east past the entrance lane to Forester's Lodge and heading towards Crag Farm.

When the lane ends at a field, cross diagonally to the left-hand corner from where you stand, heading towards a clump of small trees. (If the field has crops in it, go around the edge). The track runs along the left-hand side of some small copses of trees and then through a gap in the edge of Crag Wood before dropping down through a field to join the lane past the entrance to Crag Farm and heading up, crossing the River Esk, to Lawns Road. On joining the road, turn left and follow your path for just less than a mile back to the carpark at Danby.

This route can be combined with either Route 12 'Danby and Fryup Dale' route or Route 14 'Glaisdale' route to provide a longer day out.

Hasty Bank from Urra. *Photo: Paul Hannon*

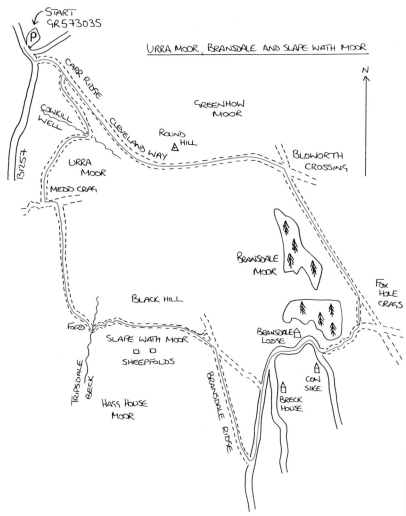

START
GR 573035

URRA MOOR, BRANSDALE AND SLAPE WATH MOOR

N

CARR RIDGE

COWKILL WELL

CLEVELAND WAY

GREENHOW MOOR

ROUND HILL

BLOWORTH CROSSING

B1257

URRA MOOR

MEDD CRAG

BRANSDALE MOOR

FOX HOLE CRAGS

BLACK HILL

FORD

SLAPE WATH MOOR

SHEEPFOLDS

TRIPSDALE BECK

HASS HOUSE MOOR

BRANSDALE RIDGE

BRANSDALE LODGE

BRECK HOUSE

COW SIKE

## 6. URRA MOOR, BRANSDALE AND SLAPE WATH MOOR

Map          – OS 26

Start point  – GR573035 Carpark at top of Clay Bank.

Distance     – 17 miles (15 miles off road/2 miles on road).

Time         – Approximately 4 hours.

GOAW factor – 4.

### Introduction:
This is a demanding ride, best suited to those who have a good level of fitness. It offers some brilliant scenery and terrain over which to travel, in return for the effort required. You will need to be wary of walkers on the Cleveland Way section, depending on the time of year and day of the week (Sundays are probably best avoided), but from Bloworth Crossing onwards you will probably be pretty much on your own until you get back to the descent from Carr Ridge to your start point. Navigation is pretty easy, with the section on Urra Moor being the one to take care around.

### The route:
From the carpark on the B1257, at the top of Clay Bank, turn left and go along the road for around a couple of hundred

yards until you see the gate on your left and the Cleveland Way acorn sign. Going through the gate, you begin the steep climb up Carr Ridge onto Urra Moor. The bridleway is very eroded on this section due to the high number of users, principally long-distance walkers, and winter rains. As it is very steep you are advised to keep to the centre of the track so as not to spread the area of wear. If this is too difficult, please get off and walk. (Great care with braking should be taken on the homeward leg of this ride, passing over the same section, so if you cannot descend without locking wheels, get off and walk down).

At the top of the ridge, the track separates and you follow the left-hand track, the Cleveland Way, in a south-easterly direction towards Round Hill and Bloworth Crossing. This is a very clear crossroads with a gate ahead of you to prevent bridleway traffic following the disused railway track around to Farndale Moor. Reaching this stage will take around 45 minutes from the start point, and should indicate around 3.7 miles if you have a computer on the bike. Having one will be useful for the next stage, when you turn right at Bloworth Crossing and follow the county road south-south-east onto Rudland Rigg. After 5.55 miles you will see a track leaving the main bridleway at around a 45 degree angle to your right. Ignore this and continue until 5.93 miles when a track will cut across your path diagonally from left to right, marked by a pile of stones on the right. Turn right here and descend towards the trees, turning to the left as you reach the trees. Go carefully down the tricky descent into Bransdale, arriving at the road near the dale head, just above Cow Sike farm.

Turn right at the road, and ride around the dale head past Bransdale Lodge and across the cattle grid. Ignore the left-hand junction to Breck House, and climb up the dale side until you see the second bridleway sign on your right, directly due west of South House Farm and at GR610964.

There is a small plaque erected by the Nawton Tower estate at the beginning of this bridleway. Follow the bridleway due north for around 1.25 miles until the track splits. You follow the left-hand fork which follows the contours around the moor side, passing two shepherd's huts, over Slape Wath Moor and heading for Tripsdale Beck. Here you will encounter a bumpy and steep descent along a four-wheel drive track which zigzags down to ford the beck. Pause at the top of this descent and look across the valley to identify your route on the other side – the clearly defined bridleway used by Estate Land Rovers which climbs in a westerly direction up to the top of Nab End Moor before turning north-west to follow the line of the earthworks along the western edge of Urra Moor towards Medd Crag.

As you approach Medd Crag, there is a T-junction in the track. You need to take the left-hand turn and begin to descend for a little while in the direction of Weighill's Plantation. Do not descend too far, and keep a lookout for the dry-stone wall heading away on your right. Although the beginning of the bridleway at this point is ill-defined, head for the wall before you drop down the last hundred yards to the gate, as this avoids you having to climb around the crags to reach the wall. If you cannot find the bridleway, do not worry – just head for the wall and after a couple of hundred yards it becomes apparent as it follows the line of the wall, on its right-hand side, and heads north back towards Carr Ridge.

This section of bridleway is not well-used, and is boggy at most times of year so should be partly walked to prevent churning up the track too much. Just under 1 mile from Medd Crag the track swings around to the right to cross a stream, before turning left again and heading towards Carr Ridge. Take care as you reach the steep drop to the stream above Cowkill Well, as you will have to carry your bike down the last few yards on the rocks and over the stream. Climbing back up from the stream you then follow the track as it climbs to meet the Cleveland Way just before the gate at the top of Carr Ridge. From there you retrace your outward route back to the carpark, taking care to prevent scarring the track as you drop steeply downhill back to the road.

Shooting butt lunch shelter. *Photo: Derek Purdy*

Stile near Cow Sike Farm. *Photo: Derek Purdy*

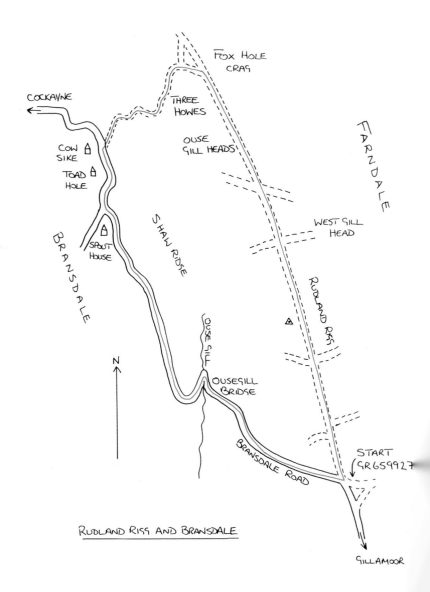

COCKAYNE

FOX HOLE CRAG

THREE HOWES

OUSE GILL HEADS

FARNDALE

COW SIKE

TOAD HOLE

WEST GILL HEAD

BRANSDALE

SHAW RIDGE

SPOUT HOUSE

RUDLAND RIGG

N

OUSE GILL

OUSEGILL BRIDGE

BRANSDALE ROAD

START (GR 659927)

RUDLAND RIGG AND BRANSDALE

GILLAMOOR

## 7. RUDLAND RIGG AND BRANSDALE

Map         – OS 26

Start point – GR659927 – Point where Westside Road joins
              the Bransdale Road.

Distance    – 11.5 miles (6.5 miles off road/5 miles on road).

Time        – Approximately 1.5 – 2 hours.

GOAW factor – 1.

**Introduction:**
We first rode the route anti-clockwise, but found it hard going
with a very long climb up Rudland Rigg, so we have written
the description in reverse as we feel it will improve the
enjoyment of the ride. The Bransdale valley is a little-visited
area as no roads actually traverse the valley. You simply
travel from Helmsley up to the valley head and then return
south to Gillamoor. The result is a very quiet and peaceful
valley with little traffic on the road section and beautiful views
towards the dale head on the outward section. There is a
hard, steep climb up from the valley onto Rudland Rigg, but
this should not take more than about 20 minutes steady
plodding and then you will enjoy great scenery looking east
over the moor tops.

**The route:**

Follow the Bransdale road north-west down towards the dale head at Cockayne. This pleasant road provides fairly easy going, arriving at Ousegill Bridge and a fun descent after some 1.5 miles. After the bridge the road turns sharply left and starts to climb steeply. Follow the road round the next sharp bend to the right as the climbing becomes more gradual. You are now climbing the lower part of Shaw Ridge. As the road gradually levels out, ignore the track forking to the right and then head downhill to the T-junction at Spout House. Here you turn right and keep to the metalled road until Cow Sike Farm.

Just after the farm you will see a gate and stile on the right-hand side of the road, leading into a pasture below the woods. Follow the steep path up the right-hand wall of the pasture, which eventually leads to a gate onto the moor. The bridleway is fairly overgrown by bracken in summer, but can still be followed easily as it rises alongside the wood. It then turns left to follow the edge of the trees under a very steep incline. As the ground to your right becomes less steep, the track veers right and then climbs towards the top of the moor, branching off to the left a few hundred yards below the summit. Keep to the right-hand track and you will arrive at the moor top opposite Fox Hole Crag.

The track you are following now reaches a crossroads of tracks. Resist the temptation of the steep descent straight ahead – the track there becomes a footpath, and only leads to a road. Instead turn right onto Westside Road, the broad, stony track running along Rudland Rigg. Head south-east in a straight line stopping at the trig point just at the side of the track to enjoy superb views to the east across Farndale, towards Blakey Ridge and Spaunton Moor. Westside Road

Trig point on Rudland Rigg

leads you in an elevated position over the top of the moors, descending slightly then climbing again over Rudland Rigg. After approx. 1.75 miles the track begins to descend and continues to do so for a couple of miles back to the Bransdale Road and the start point.

This route can be combined with the route no. 8 'Rudland Rigg and Farndale', to provide a longer day out.

# RUDLAND RIGG AND FARNDALE

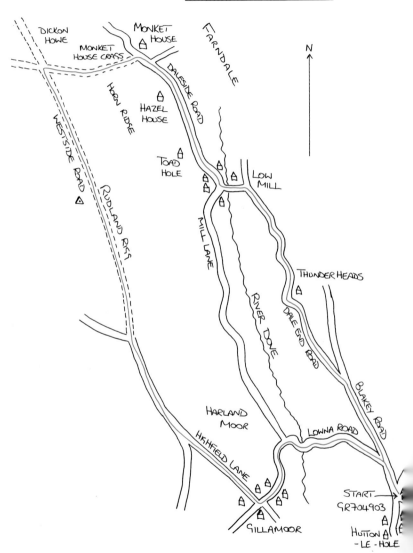

## 8. RUDLAND RIGG AND FARNDALE

Map            – OS 26

Start point    – GR704902 – Carpark in Hutton-le-Hole.

Distance       – Total 19 miles (5 miles off road/14 miles on road).

Time           – Approximately 2.5 hours.

GOAW factor – 1.

**Introduction:**
Most of the hard work is done on the road section at the beginning of this ride. The ride is generally quite a strenuous one, although without any major obstacles to overcome – the road which climbs up to Gillamoor probably being the worst of the lot. The return leg, through Farndale, is very scenic and takes you over the River Dove – haunt of billions of once a year moors visitors in the spring when the famous Farndale daffodils are in flower along the river banks. Watch out for the tourist coaches at this time of year as they take up all of the narrow roads and you can end up eating hawthorn hedge or closely inspecting dry-stone walling!

**The route:**
From the carpark, turn right onto Keld Lane and then first left

on to Lowna Road, heading for Gillamoor. The road descends crossing first Shortsha Beck and then the River Dove. Climb up the hill to arrive at Gillamoor where you get a fine view over your route so far. Continue on this road through the village and at the end of the village turn right onto Highfield Lane. Follow the lane as it climbs steadily north-west, passing Dial Farm and several other farms before climbing out onto more open moorland. Approx. 2 miles from Gillamoor, the lane forks left at a junction. Here you continue straight on, almost due north, climbing up the track which runs along Rudland Rigg.

This track climbs up to Golden Heights (376m), descends slightly and then climbs again. Follow the track ignoring all paths to right and left. After around 3.5 miles you will see a clearly marked track crossing your path diagonally from right to left, GR641975. This is marked on the map as a track descending the hill, to the south of Dickon Howe, and heading for Monket House.

Although there are no green bridleway markings on the map this is in fact an old county road so you do have right of way – care should be taken on the lower sections where the surface is eroded and there is a steep drop on your left. The road follows the contours of the hillside now, heading roughly south-east. Continue on the road until you reach Low Mill. At the T-junction in Low Mill, turn left and then soon right onto Daleside Road. Continue travelling south-east past Thunderheads. Less than 2 miles further on you come to a junction where your road meets Blakey Road. Turn right here and enjoy the gradual descent into Hutton-le-Hole and the start point.

This route can be combined with the previous route (no. 7) 'Rudland Rigg and Bransdale' to provide a longer day out.

Farndale. *Photo: Paul Hannon*

Fit padding to make carrying less uncomfortable

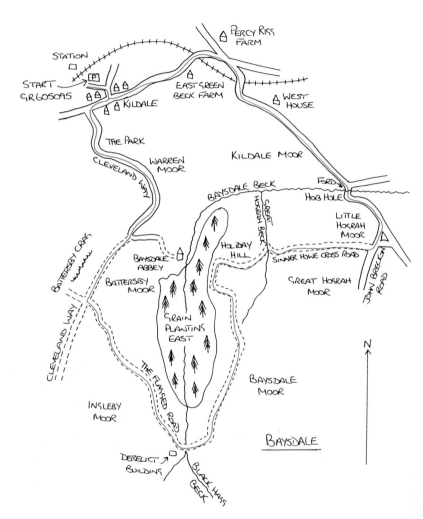

BAYSDALE

58

## 9.  BAYSDALE

Map            — OS 26

Start point    — GR605095 – The village of Kildale (parking near
                 Kildale Station).

Distance       — Total 13.5 miles (8 miles off road/5.5 miles on
                 road).

Time           — Approximately 3 hours.

GOAW factor — 3-4.

**Introduction:**
This ride is demanding both physically and in terms of
navigation. You traverse some very unused moorland in
which you are unlikely to come across anyone else, so
equipment needs to be in good order before you set off. We
spent around half an hour replacing lost toeclip bolts and
straightening handlebars twisted on the descent to Armouth
Wath – from experience we can advise that you do not want
to be sat around in exposed surroundings in which you cool
down fast. So make sure everything is really tight before you
set off. The views are spectacular on this ride and the climbs
at the end are pretty punishing, but overall it is a ride which
will leave you feeling that you have accomplished something.

**The route:**

From Kildale, head west and take the first road on your left which follows the Cleveland Way. This climbs due south, then south-east, up onto Warren Moor. The road presents a steep climb at first, becoming more gradual as you follow it round to the right, heading south again. After 2 miles on tarmac the road turns sharp left, and you continue straight ahead along the bridleway directly in front of you. Follow this in a straight line up onto Battersby Moor for around 0.5 miles. You then turn left, leaving the Cleveland Way, and heading south-east over Ingleby Moor toward Armouth Wath.

After about 0.5 miles you cross a small beck and then climb again. Go straight over the junction of tracks on what is now called the Flagged Road. Before descending and crossing the beck at Armouth Wath, look across to the other side of the valley and spot the bridleway rising around the side of the hill and turning northwards – this will help you head in the right direction from the bottom of the beck, where you lose sight of the track briefly. Basically you need to climb up from the beck in more or less a straight line from the direction you descended on the other side, then turn left to head north.

You now cross Baysdale Moor almost due north. After another 1.5 miles the track parts and the bridleway you follow veers left to arrive at the plantation to the east of Baysdale Abbey. Follow the bridleway along the margins of the woodlands, until it turns sharp right away from the woods. You will see an old fence in front of you up the hill, heading right to left for the small summit of Holiday Hill. Cross the fence, skirting to the south of the hilltop and follow the bridleway east.

You are now heading towards Skinner Howe Cross Road and crossing Great Hograh Moor, which can be very muddy

Battersby Moor

Hob Hole. *Photo: Derek Purdy*

after rain – keep to the centre of the track to avoid further erosion. Take care approaching Great Hograh Beck, as you will need to cross the beck on foot and there is a sharp drop off just before the beck. Climb up again onto Great Hograh Moor crossing it eastwards then descending slightly as you cross Little Hograh Moor. Still descending, you will come to John Breckon Road, a tarmac surface, which connects with the road heading north-west out of Westerdale.

Turn left and then left again and follow this road north-west, descending to Hob Hole. Cross the ford and follow the road as it gets steeper. Go straight over the crossroads of tracks and start the hard climb up across Kildale Moor. Follow this road over the moor and then begin the descent towards Kildale. After crossing the railway you enter Crag Bank Wood. On the other side of the wood turn left onto the road which takes you back into Kildale and the start point.

Mill Bank Wood. *Photo: Derek Purdy*

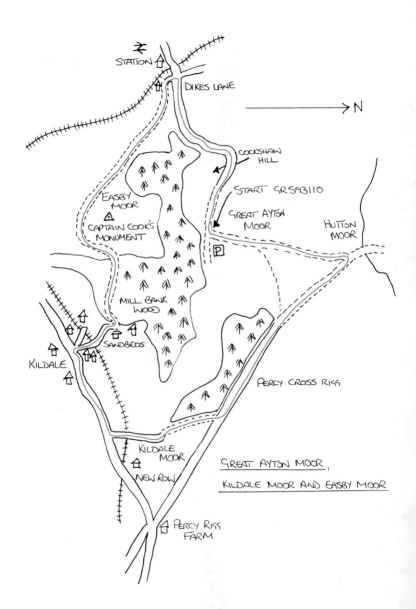

STATION

DIKES LANE

→ N

COCKSHAW HILL

START GR 593110

EASBY MOOR

CAPTAIN COOK'S MONUMENT

GREAT AYTON MOOR

HUTTON MOOR

P

MILL BANK WOOD

SANDBEDS

KILDALE

PERCY CROSS RIGG

KILDALE MOOR

NEW ROW

PERCY RIGG FARM

GREAT AYTON MOOR,

KILDALE MOOR AND EASBY MOOR

## 10. GREAT AYTON MOOR, KILDALE MOOR AND EASBY MOOR

Map           – OS 26

Start point   – GR593110 – Carpark below Cockshaw Hill, accessed from Station Road, Great Ayton, along Dikes Lane and right after Gribdale Terrace.

Distance      – 9 miles (6.5 miles off road/2.5 miles on road).

Time          – Approximately 1.75 hours.

GOAW factor – 1.

**Introduction:**
This is a shorter ride, especially suitable if you do not have a lot of time, and offers a good mix of terrain and fairly simple navigation. The area around the start seems popular with a lot of the local mountain bike racing fraternity who obviously use it as a practice area – but do not let the expensive machinery and dayglo silly suits put you off, just get plodding off up that first hill and leave them to it. There is a fair climb to begin with, but the rest of the ride is easy going apart from the last hike back up to the carpark area.

**The route:**
From the carpark, head east then almost due north on the signposted bridleway up the steep hill onto Great Ayton

Moor. The bridleway you should follow becomes very indistinct, but heads towards GR598128 in just over 1 mile – just below Hutton Lowcross Woods on Hutton Moor. Here you turn sharp right and head south-east along Percy Cross Rigg across Kildale Moor. (There is an obvious track which cuts off this corner, heading from the top of Great Ayton Moor in a big arc towards the northern point of Lonsdale Plantation. Do not be tempted to take this route, as it is designated as a footpath only).

From the top of Lonsdale Plantation follow the forestry road to the end of the plantation and turn right, now following the eastern edge of the plantation due south. The track eventually crosses a narrow section of the plantation and you emerge just above New Row, on Quarry Hill. Go straight on, over the railway line and down to the main road, where you turn right to Kildale. On entering the village you join the Cleveland Way by taking the first right, then right again. Cross the railway line and head into Sandbeds Plantation. At the end of the tarmac section, when you reach the farm buildings, take the woodland bridleway to your left. This takes you through Mill Bank Wood following the contours of the hillside below Easby Moor (and is also marked with blue arrows). You soon come out onto the open hillside below Captain Cook's Monument. Unfortunately you cannot see the monument from your position – your best view is from the top of Great Ayton Moor at the start of the ride – but the view from up there is worth a walk up from the carpark after your ride.

From below the monument, follow the track north-west entering more woodland then following the edge of Ayton Banks Wood on your right. After leaving the wood you start to descend to Southbrook Farm. At the farm turn right onto Dikes Lane, heading back up the steep hill to the carpark.

Roseberry Topping from Newton Moor. *Photo: Paul Hannon*

Some worthwhile equipment

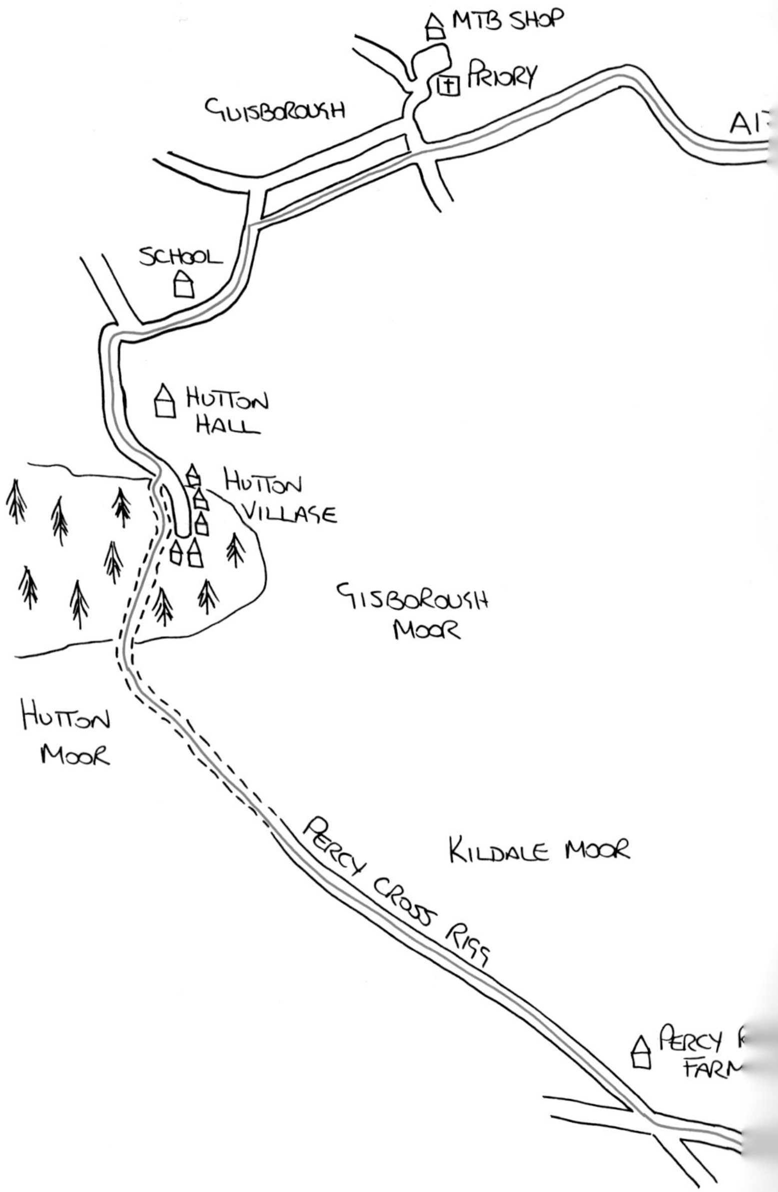

MTB SHOP

PRIORY

GUISBOROUGH

AI

SCHOOL

HUTTON HALL

HUTTON VILLAGE

GISBOROUGH MOOR

HUTTON MOOR

PERCY CROSS RIGG

KILDALE MOOR

PERCY F FARM

# COMMONDALE AND GISBOROUGH MOORS

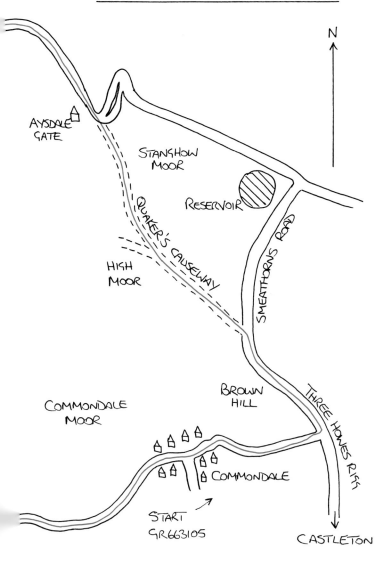

AYSDALE GATE

STANGHOW MOOR

RESERVOIR

QUAKER'S CAUSEWAY

HIGH MOOR

SMEATHORNS ROAD

N

BROWN HILL

THREE HOWES RIGG

COMMONDALE MOOR

COMMONDALE

START
GR663105

CASTLETON

## 11.  COMMONDALE AND GISBOROUGH MOORS

Map            – OS 26

Start point    – GR663105 – The village of Commondale.

Distance       – 16 miles (4 miles off road/12 miles on road).

Time           – Approximately 2.5 – 3 hours.

GOAW factor – 3.

### Introduction:
This is an interesting and varied ride, especially for those with
a liking for history, as it partly follows one of the ancient
pannierman's causeways – paved "roads" along which laden
pack animals were led in former times – and also passes close
by Guisborough Priory, worth a visit if only for the peace and
quiet away from the traffic of this busy market town. The
going is fairly mixed, with a couple of longish walks, but with
the compensation of some long descents and some very
attractive scenery over Kildale Moor on the homeward
section.

### The route:
From Commondale, head east out of the village towards
Three Howes Rigg. When you arrive at the T-junction turn left
and start the climb up Brown Hill. Just after the top of the hill

the road swings right, due north. Here you leave the road and follow the Quaker's Causeway north-west across High Moor. This is an old paved track and you will soon reach the part on which the old flagstones are exposed. You are able to ride alongside the flagstones for much of the way – be careful not to scrape metal pedals on the stones if climbing onto the stones over certain sections, as the sandstone will be easily marked and damaged. At the first junction in the track, take the right-hand fork towards Woodhill Gill Head. You now descend, crossing a few small becks which feed the reservoir on your right. On reaching Woodhill Gill Head take the left-hand fork to descend along the eastern side of Woodhill Gill towards the main road at Aysdale Gate.

A couple of notes of caution: when we did the ride there were horses in the fields above the farm, so go slowly so as not to spook them; and when you reach the concreted track immediately before the main road do not hang about near the farmhouse garden wall as there were a couple of very interested, very large hounds that could not get over the wall, but left you in no doubt as to what would happen if they could! Fortunately the farm garden is immediately next to the main road on a big downhill section so you can be off at high speed if you are nervous about dogs. Be careful about joining the road as cars travel downhill at a fair speed.

Turn left onto the A171 and follow it over 2 miles right into Guisborough itself. You should pause for a while at the Priory. Here you will find a pub, sandwich shop and a very good MTB shop tucked into the corner of the Priory carpark. To reach these, turn right at the first set of lights you reach in Guisborough, and then next right – the Priory carpark is a hundred yards or so around the bend on your right.

Continuing on from here – go back to the traffic lights you

71

first reached, turn right along the road past the car and coach parks until reaching a T-junction where you turn left. Follow the road along until it turns sharp right towards the A173, and you continue straight on towards Hutton Village.

As the road swings round to the left you enter the parkland approach to the village. Just before the first houses you will see a bridleway on the right which climbs into the woods behind the gardens of the houses. Follow the bridleway upwards into Blue Lake Wood and Hutton Wood. Continue in a straight line all the way uphill to the top of the woods where you emerge onto Hutton Moor. The track is easy to follow as it is very broad and has obviously been used by four-wheel drive vehicles and motorcycles. You will almost certainly end up walking up the steeper sections – the only problem with this being the midges and flies to be found in the warmer months in the woodlands.

Riding out of the woods you will find an easy track heading south-east across Hutton Moor. Follow this over a short initial climb and then relax on the descent to join the metalled road along Percy Cross Rigg. The road takes you past Lonsdale Plantation on your right and then climbs over Brown Hill. After about 1.5 miles you pass Percy Rigg Farm on your left. Soon after the farm you reach a crossroads. Turn left here and drop down the steep hill to the cattle grid. Take a deep breath and pedal up the hard climb on the other side. This soon levels out and you can rest your muscles on the easy descent back down into Commondale and the start point.

Guisborough Priory

Bridleway signs used on the N. Yorks Moors

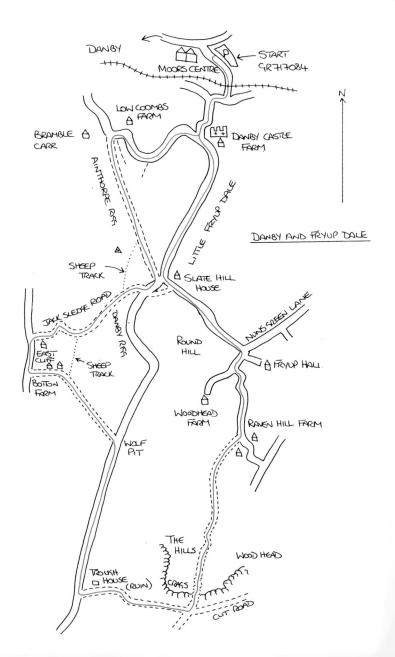

# EASTERN AREA

## 12. DANBY AND FRYUP DALE

Map — OS 27

Start point — GR717084 — Carpark of The Moors Centre at Danby.

Distance — Total 12 miles (5.8 off road/6.2 on road).

Time — Approximately 2 – 2.5 hours.

GOAW factor — 1.

**Introduction:**
This is one of the best routes in the book as far as scenery and variety of riding are concerned, and should not prove too taxing in terms of map reading for anyone. The going is pretty easy, with only a couple of sections where you will need to walk. We have marked on the map a couple of sheep tracks on Danby Rigg which follow the contours of the hillside across where the bridleways drop down and ascend again, but these are only to aid navigation – do not be tempted to short-cut the official route by walking along them, as they are not a right of way.

The Moors Centre at Danby, the start of the ride, is well worth a visit as it gives the new visitor to the North York Moors a great insight into the area and you can lay your hands on all sorts of information – as well as a cold drink or a cup of tea when the café is open.

**The route:**
Leaving the carpark, turn left and follow the road south. It passes under the railway bridge and comes to a T-junction, where you turn right. Cross the River Esk and then turn left towards Danby Castle. The road splits just before Danby Castle Farm and you take the right-hand road towards Low Coombs Farm. Just after a footpath marker on your left, before reaching the farm, you will see a bridleway also on the left which climbs up on to Ainthorpe Rigg. Follow this bridleway up the hill, riding due south. You then descend Crossley Side to meet the roads from Little Fryup Dale and Danby where they meet at a T-junction just south of Slate Hill House.

Turn right, uphill, onto New Way for a few hundred yards, before following another bridleway to your right – Jack Sledge Road. This climbs up Danby Rigg in a south-westerly direction, crosses the top of the hill and zigzags down the other side. On reaching the lane, turn left and follow the hillside south until you meet another bridleway. Take this and climb back up the hill to meet the Danby road again at Wolf Pit. (If you do not want to incur this extra climb, continue south along New Way from Slate Hill House for about 1.5 miles to the bridleway turning by Trough House.)

Turn right and follow the road south for just over a mile. Then turn left onto a bridleway past Trough House, due east, to the dale head at GR714017. Turn left here, taking care to identify the area of the cliff head that projects furthest into the dale, as this is the only place to begin your descent. If you are unsure, follow the bridleway from a small sign on your right which says "bridleway", until you have crossed 2 main stream paths falling into the dale to your left. Then turn left and you should be able to see that you are following a clearly

Great Fryup Head. *Photo: Paul Hannon*

defined track which approaches the cliff top and then zigzags down the cliff on a track which is 2–3 feet wide. **IMPORTANT – do not attempt to ride any of this descent, as any loss of control would leave you open to a nasty fall.** At the base of the cliffs, head to the left of the dale and cross the stream. You can see the track on the left-hand side which takes you to the road at Raven Hill Farm. Turn left on the road and follow it north past another farm on your right. Climb up to a point where the road turns sharp right and follow it round to a T-junction. Turn left here and climb up again through a wooded area. Follow the road now heading north-west past Stone Beck Gate Farm to the T-junction you previously met at Slate Hill House. Turn right here and continue under Crossley Side on Castle Lane. When you have passed Danby Castle again, take the first turn right, then right again, finally turning left under the railway line to retrace your ride back to the carpark at Danby and the start point.

Note: In bad weather or poor visibility, the cliff descent could prove difficult for some people. It should not be attempted if you are not absolutely sure that you are on the correct track. If the track down the cliff is seen as too steep a descent for anyone in the party, continue to follow the dale head bridleway for approx. 1.5 miles until it meets the road which runs along Glaisdale Rigg. Turn left here and follow the road for just over 1 mile until you can turn left again and descend into Great Fryup Dale. Keep left all the time until you reach Raven Hill Farm, and rejoin the route as above.

Milestone on Pannierman's Causeway (to Whitby?) *Photo: Derek Purdy*

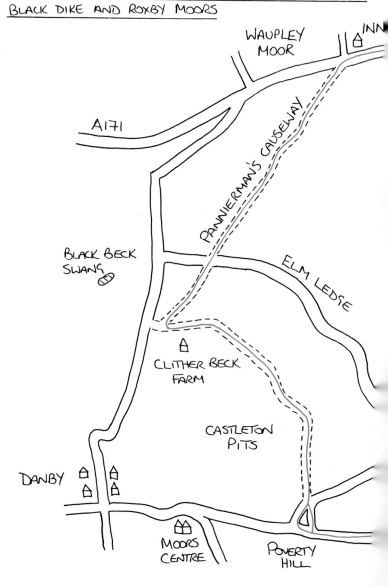

WAUPLEY MOOR

INN

A171

PANNIERMAN'S CAUSEWAY

ELM LEDGE

BLACK BECK SWANS

CLITHER BECK FARM

CASTLETON PITS

DANBY

MOORS CENTRE

POVERTY HILL

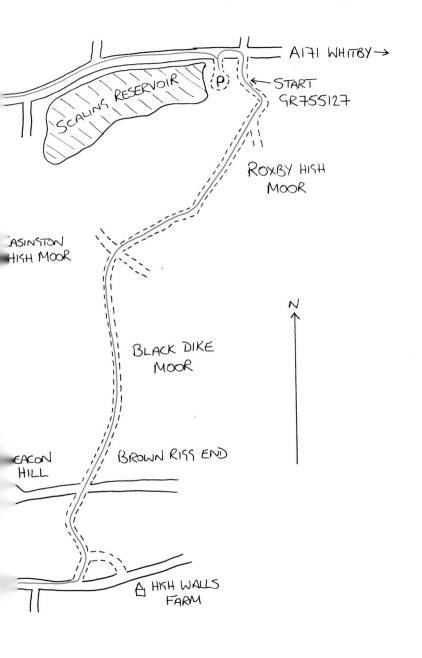

## 13. SCALING RESERVOIR, EASINGTON HIGH MOOR, LEALHOLM, BLACK DIKE AND ROXBY MOORS

Map          – OS 27

Start point  – GR755127 – Scaling Dam Reservoir carpark.

Distance     – 10.5 miles (7.5 off road/3 on road).

Time         – Approximately 2 hours.

GOAW factor – 1.

**Introduction:**
If nothing else, this ride has the longest title description in the book, passing over a large number of smaller moors which are really indistinguishable from one another. Navigation is difficult over several sections, although anyone encountering problems will not come to much harm as there are plenty of roads crossing the area. The end of the ride offers a challenge in compass work and map reading as there is very little evidence of the route actually visible. This part can be avoided if you are not happy with the prospect of wading knee-high through the heather and gorse which abounds on this section. The physical side is not bad, and very little walking is required due to gradient, but more down to a poor riding surface.

**The route:**
From the carpark at the eastern end of Scaling Dam Reservoir turn right towards the A171. When you reach the road turn right and head east on the road for 100 metres. Take the next right turn onto a lane which heads due south. Where the lane forks you take the bridleway on the right which climbs gently onto Roxby High Moor. Follow the track right across the moor until you meet a hard core track a few hundred yards east of Danby Beacon.

Cross straight over this track, heading south-west for a few hundred yards prior to turning due south again and heading for the Danby road. The bridleway becomes very indistinct around here, and the moor is usually boggy; following a course due south will bring you out on the road within a short distance of the bridleway marker. The bridleway forks just before the road – take the right fork, turn right onto the road and follow it to the first road to your right. Take this turning and climb up to a T-junction with an old stone gatepost on the right. From the T-junction, continue straight on along another bridleway which travels above Castleton Pits and towards Clither Beck Farm.

As you ride above Clither Beck Farm, and just before arriving at the road heading north out of Danby, turn right in a north-easterly direction along Pannierman's Causeway. You should follow this bridleway, crossing over the dead-end road to Danby Beacon. After crossing the small beck of Sandy Slack you come to a junction of bridleways. Go straight ahead (north-west) and after 0.5 miles you reach the main A171 road opposite the inn on Waupley Moor. Turn right onto the main road and follow it back until you reach Scaling Dam Reservoir and the carpark.

**Note**: Pannierman's Causeway is extremely indistinct in parts, and not very rideable. If weather conditions are poor or any of the party is fatigued, you are strongly advised to follow the road route back to Scaling Dam Reservoir by continuing down to the road after Clither Beck Farm then turning right and right again on the A171.

Crossing the beck at Clither Beck Farm. *Photo: Derek Purdy*

Toll Board, Egton Bridge. *Photo: Paul Hannon*

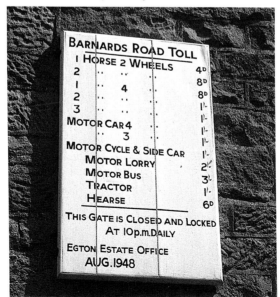

BARNARDS ROAD TOLL

| | | |
|---|---|---|
| 1 HORSE 2 WHEELS | | 4ᴅ |
| 2 ,, ,, | | 8ᴅ |
| 1 ,, 4 ,, | | 8ᴅ |
| 2 ,, ,, | | 1/- |
| 3 ,, ,, | | 1/- |
| MOTOR CAR 4 ,, | | 1/- |
| ,, 3 ,, | | 1/- |
| MOTOR CYCLE & SIDE CAR | | 1/- |
| MOTOR LORRY | | 2/- |
| MOTOR BUS | | 3/- |
| TRACTOR | | 1/- |
| HEARSE | | 6ᴅ |

THIS GATE IS CLOSED AND LOCKED
AT 10 p.m. DAILY

EGTON ESTATE OFFICE
AUG. 1948

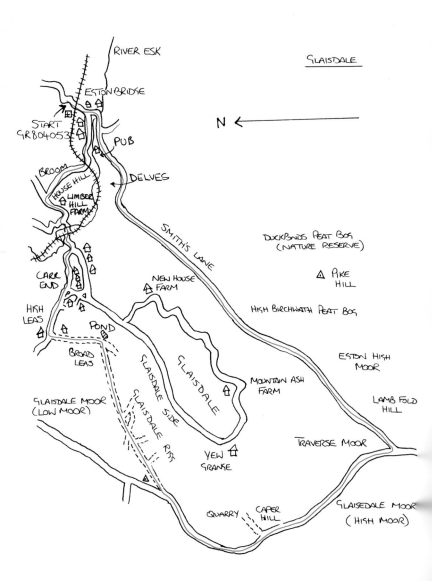

## 14. GLAISDALE

Map          – OS 27

Start point  – GR804053 – Carpark next to church in Egton
                Bridge.

Distance     – 14.5 miles (2.5 off road/12 miles on road).

Time         – Approximately 3 hours.

GOAW factor – 3.

**Introduction:**
A physical outward section, rewarding high moor surroundings and a big descent on the way back sum up this ride.
There is plenty to keep you interested on the early stages
where you move up and down the hilly contours of Eskdale,
and amazing views towards Whitby from the higher sections
of Glaisdale Rigg as you climb up to the higher stages. The
return route is all road work but traffic tends to be fairly light
in this area as the major north-south routes run to either side
of these valleys. It is an easy route to follow and a fairly good
one for beginners who might prefer an easier surface on
which to pedal.

**The route:**
From the carpark, turn right down the hill and immediately

right again, heading west on the road to Glaisdale village and following the course of the River Esk. Passing under the railway line you begin the first steep climb up Broom House Lane to a T-junction. Turn left here and descend round a sharp right then sharp left bend and under the railway again into the hamlet of Carr End.

Climbing up through Carr End, take the right-hand turn opposite the garage. Then begin the steep climb up into Glaisdale village via the back lane. Soon you arrive at the main road again opposite the Mitre Inn. Turn right here and head out of the village, past the green. A little over 0.5 miles further on you reach High Leas. From here you take the bridleway on your right-hand side opposite High Leas, leaving the road to your left. This point is 3.5 miles from the start point and most of the hard work has been done by this stage.

Heading south past Broad Leas, you follow the bridleway up onto Glaisdale Moor until you reach a boggy pond where 4 tracks meet. Turn right here and continue to the next junction. Leave the bridleway and take the right-hand track which gently climbs along Glaisdale Rigg. Continue on this track for around 2 miles until you meet the road heading south from Lealholm.

Turn left onto the road, following it across Glaisdale High Moor. This is pleasant, easy riding and you follow it for about 3 miles, around the Glaisdale valley head until it meets the road from Rosedale on Traverse Moor. This junction is signposted to show that you have 5 miles still to go back into Egton Bridge. Turning left at this junction, follow the road past, on your left Wintergill Plantation, and on your right High Birchwath Peat Bog and the nature reserve of Duckponds Peat Bog on Egton High Moor.

On Glaisedale Rigg. *Photo: Derek Purdy*

Going past the grouse butts alongside the road, you commence the very steep and fast descent over the last couple of miles along Smith's Lane passing by the wooded area around Delves. Some of the corners at the bottom of the hill are pretty tight and gravel-strewn, and can be dangerous at high speed – you have been warned. The descent eases out as you near Egton Bridge. Go past the Horseshoe Inn and back up the hill to your start point.

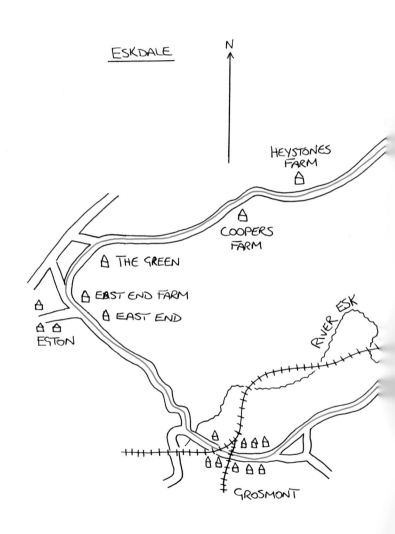

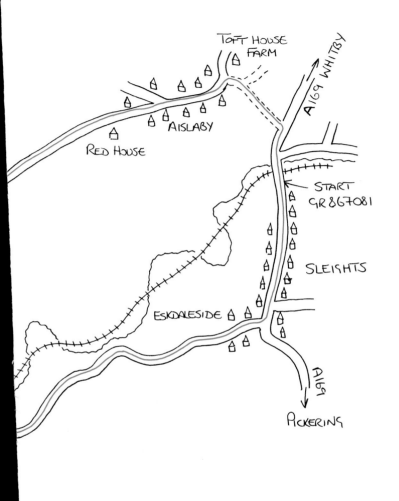

## 15. ESKDALE

Map          – OS 27

Start point  – GR867081 – Carpark in Sleights.

Distance     – 11.5 miles (virtually all on road).

Time         – Approximately 1.5 hours.

GOAW factor – 3.

**Introduction:**
This is the only all road route in the guide, and is probably a good introduction for anyone new to mountain biking, who needs to get used to gradients and using their gears and brakes, prior to getting off road when more concentration is required for the surface in front of you and your orienteering.

The major drawback of this route is the size of the climb up from Grosmont, but if you view this as good training for later rides it might not seem such a waste of effort. Besides, the views from the top are very pleasant, and once up to the top of the Eskdale valley side you can virtually coast the rest of the ride.

**The route:**
From the carpark in Sleights, head uphill (south) towards Pickering on the A169. At the top of the village turn right

along the road signposted to Grosmont – along Eskdaleside.

The road climbs and descends fairly frequently along this stretch, but the view down into the valley should distract you from the climbs. You cross over several becks and pass by as many farms, continuing on the road for about 2 miles until you reach the steep drop into Grosmont. Here concentration on the road is required (we clocked 40 mph!).

Descend into Grosmont, ignoring the left turn just before the village. Cross the railway lines in Grosmont and then follow the same road back out of the village. Just after crossing the River Esk you come to a junction at Priory Farm, where you follow your road round to the left. Now, unfortunately you will have to begin the serious climb (walk) up towards Egton, approximately a mile further up the hill. You reach the top of the hill just by the first buildings in Egton and with delight realise that all of the work is over.

Do not continue into the village of Egton but take the first lane on the right. Follow this lane past East End Farm on your right soon to arrive at a T-junction. Turn right onto the lane which follows the valley side and provides fine views of the Eskdale valley – just reward for such a hard climb. A little under one mile further on, the road forks with a bridleway, at Cooper's Farm. Follow the road right, down a quick descent to continue following the contours of the valley side.

After 2 miles on this road you arrive at the village of Aislaby. Continue straight on through the village on the road which joins yours from the left. When you have nearly reached the end of Aislaby village and the road is about to turn left, look for a lane going straight ahead downhill, signposted "Featherbed Lane". This is your bridleway route back down to Sleights. Follow this for around a hundred yards before turning right and continuing down the hill until

93

Looking towards Whitby from Aislaby

you reach the main A169 at the bottom. This lane is partially paved with old-fashioned slabs and should be ridden with caution in the wet. At the A169 turn right to return to the start point in Sleights.

Feather Bed Lane. *Photo: Derek Purdy*

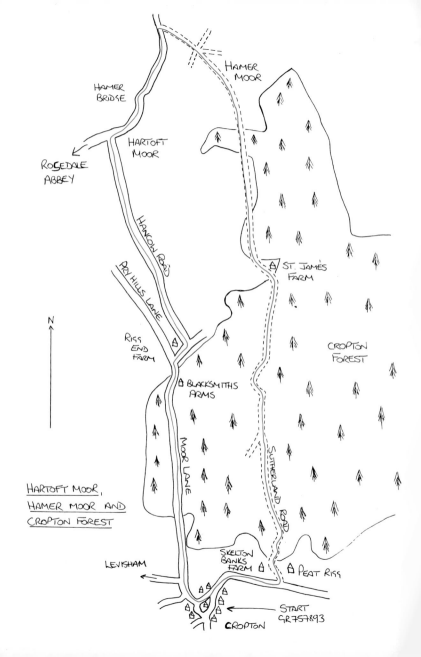

HAMER
MOOR

HAMER
BRIDGE

HARTOFT
MOOR

ROSEDALE
ABBEY

HANCOW ROAD

PEY HILLS LANE

N

RISS
END
FARM

St. JAMES
FARM

CROPTON
FOREST

BLACKSMITHS
ARMS

MOOR LANE

SUTHERLAND ROAD

HARTOFT MOOR,
HAMER MOOR AND
CROPTON FOREST

LEVISHAM

SKELTON
BANKS
FARM

PEAT RISS

START
GR 757893

CROPTON

## 16. HARTOFT MOOR, HAMER MOOR AND CROPTON FOREST

Map          – OS 27

Start point  – GR757893 – The village of Cropton.

Distance     – 16.5 miles (8 miles off road/8.5 miles on road).

Time         – Approximately 3.5 hours.

GOAW factor – 3.

**Introduction:**
This ride starts in the village of Cropton, near Pickering. It takes in the eastern side of Rosedale and some excellent fast downhills back through Cropton Forest. A very enjoyable ride, with plenty of forestry riding which provides good shelter and a bit of variety from the more exposed moor which features in most of these routes. It is another route which, due to the forestry machinery operating in the woodlands, is best left for dry weather when the surface is less chewed up and boggy.

If you try this route in late summer you will see lots of curlews and lapwings which nest on Hamer Moor and take noisy exception to anyone riding along the road from Hamer Bridge. There is not a great deal of walking involved, and what there is appears mainly on the outbound section on metalled roads. Navigation is pretty easy, with a bit of care needing to be taken in Cropton Forest. This is a good confidence building route for intermediate riders.

**The route:**

From Cropton, head through the village southwards, turning right – due north – on Moor Lane towards Rosedale Abbey. Cross Cropton Beck on Cropton Bridge and continue due north heading towards the forest. The road runs along-side the forest for a short while and then enters it at Blackpark Lodge. After 2.25 miles you emerge from the forest to cross the River Seven at Hartoft Bridge. Soon after you arrive at Hartoft End. After passing the Blacksmith's Arms at Hartoft End, take the next road on the right and then turn first left after Rigg End Farm. This section is the worst of the uphills. (This ride is mainly uphill on the outbound section and downhill virtually all the way back.)

The lane takes you through two small plantations, along Hancow Road. After a couple of miles it meets the road coming up from Rosedale Abbey. Turn right here and descend to Hamer Bridge, followed by a climb of around 1 mile to the bridleway which crosses the road.

Turn right at the bridleway, and ride south-east over Hamer Moor towards the top north-west section of Cropton Forest. As you travel along the first section of the bridleway there is a dry-stone wall on your left-hand side. When you come to the end of this the track visibly splits three ways and you need to follow the central track. This descends a rough track towards the woods. When you reach the beck just before the woods the bridleway actually crosses the beck and follows the left-hand side down to a gate into the woods.

The first part of the track is fairly boggy and unrideable but

Young enthusiasts under the chestnut tree at Cropton. *Photo: Derek Purdy*

Sutherland Road in Cropton Forest.

improves after the section marked "sheepfold" on the OS map, at GR762959 – from then on it has a fairly good surface. You should note that the section shown on the OS map between GR762964 and GR763959 as open ground is actually fully covered by trees on your left-hand side – so do not think that you are off track.

After passing St. James's Farm, the track continues south for around a mile. It then swings left and slightly uphill to a T-junction. Turn right here and ride downhill for a few hundred yards. Look out for a fork in the road with a marker post behind you on the right. This indicates the actual line of the bridleway through the trees crossing your track to take the left-hand fork (GR764928). (Use a compass to determine south if you are not sure which is the correct track when you reach the fork. Even if you take the wrong track you will only end up on the road taken on your outbound leg which can be taken left back to Cropton.)

Ignore the big downhill directly in front of you and take the left fork which then takes you along Sutherland Road to Skelton Banks Farm. The last part of the track is a steep tarmac hill. Climb up past the farm to a T-junction with a road, High Lane. Turn right and follow the road for 1.25 miles to a sharp left turn, which then leads you back to Cropton and the start point.

The turnoff onto Hamer Moor. *Photo: Derek Purdy*

*Wheeldale Roman Road. Photo: Paul Hannon*

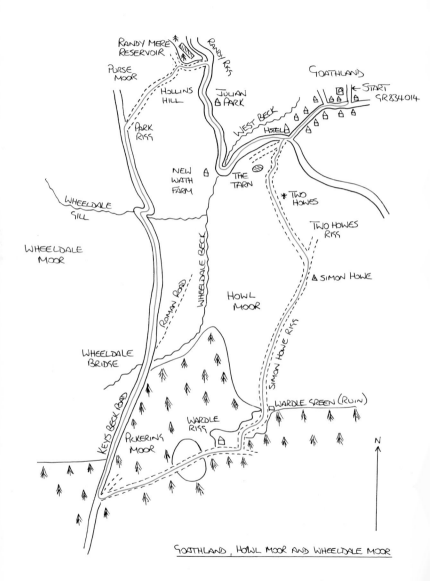

GOATHLAND, HOWL MOOR AND WHEELDALE MOOR

## 17. GOATHLAND, HOWL MOOR AND WHEELDALE MOOR

Map          – OS 27

Start point  – GR834013 – Carpark in Goathland village.

Distance    – 13 miles (5.5 miles off road/7.5 miles on road).

Time         – Approximately 3 – 3.5 hours.

GOAW factor – 3.

**Introduction:**
This is a technically difficult ride in terms of route finding, and offers a challenge in riding terrain as well. The early part of the route offers great views over the high moors. Narrow track riding, with navigation aided by a few, hard to spot marker posts provides a puzzle. As with other more difficult routes, you cannot go too far wrong but it is rewarding to be accurate in your navigation and arrive at exactly the right spot on your map – so take time to study the terrain and make the right choices based on your compass, map and intuition. There are only a couple of places where you may need to walk, notably the Wheeldale Road area where you will find a couple of steep hills.

**The route:**
From the carpark in Goathland, head south through the village towards the Mallyan Spout Hotel then turn right at the road junction just after the hotel. The bridleway leaves the road on your left a few yards after the road junction, and heads due south up the hill towards The Tarn – a small lake which you pass along its left-hand side. Do note that the bridleway splits just off the road and you need to take the left-hand fork, heading towards Two Howes and the trig point at GR832982.

There are several different tracks across Two Howes Rigg. It will help you if you aim to keep to the right of Two Howes – the two small tumuli seen ahead of you, and to the right of the trig point above Simon Howes. There are marker posts at intervals along the moor displaying the blue arrow denoting a bridleway, and you should look for these to stay on the correct track. As you look ahead from Simon Howes, identify the gap in the woodlands in front of you where you will be aiming to climb up the gentle incline to Wardle Rigg. As you descend the moor towards Blawath Beck, there is a gate in the bottom left-hand side of the field. This gives you access to the bridleway through the fields to the farm access road which you join just east of Wardle Rigg.

Turn right onto the track and ride along Brown Howe Road. This road takes you south-west past Brown Howe and then through the forest. After 1.75 miles you arrive at the junction at Mauley Cross. Turn right onto Keys Beck Road and ride north following the edge of the forest. Another 1.75 miles from Mauley Cross and you arrive at Wheeldale Bridge, crossing over Wheeldale Beck. Continue travelling due north on Wheeldale Road for another 1.5 miles where the road begins to descend more steeply towards a ford over

Elter Beck near Goathland.

Wheeldale Gill.

After crossing the ford climb the steep hill towards Park Rigg. Take the first bridleway on your right which leads you over Park Rigg and Hollins Hill towards the right-hand edge of the plantation surrounding Randy Mere Reservoir. As you cross Hollins Hill the bridleway becomes very indistinct. You should be looking ahead to identify the tree line marking the plantation and use your best judgement to arrive at the dry-stone wall surrounding the plantation. The real track heads south-west on the map so keep to that direction.

There is a very decrepit gate in the left-hand corner of the field adjoining the plantation and this should be crossed with extreme care to avoid injury to yourself and further damage to the gate. Follow the wall through the field to the bottom left-hand corner where you will find another high gate which needs to be climbed. You then drop sharply downhill to cross a small valley and climb up to the road opposite Thackside Farm. Turn right onto the road and follow this south to the small hamlet of Julian Park. Go straight on and continue on the road as it descends to a bridge over West Beck. The road now turns north-west and climbs back up from the ford, flattens out again and leads you back to Goathland.

Looking towards Fylingdales from Two Howes

Goathland. *Photo: Paul Hannon*

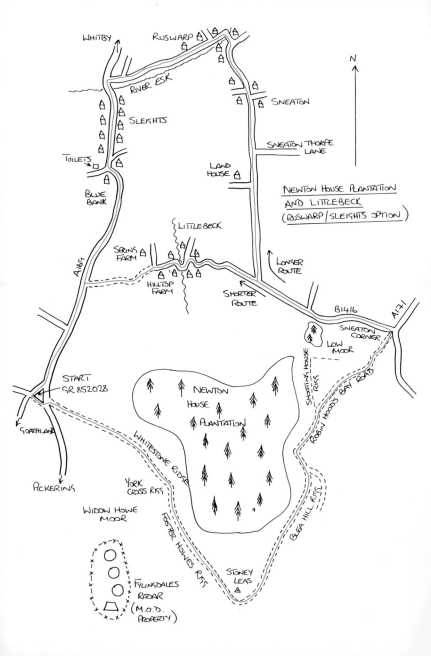

WHITBY

RUSWARP

RIVER ESK

SLEIGHTS

TOILETS

BLUE BANK

SNEATON

SNEATON THORPE LANE

LAND HOUSE

N

NEWTON HOUSE PLANTATION
AND LITTLEBECK
(RUSWARP/SLEIGHTS OPTION)

LITTLEBECK

A169

SPRING FARM

HILLTOP FARM

LONGER ROUTE

SHORTER ROUTE

B1416

A171

SNEATON CORNER

LOW MOOR

SHOSTINS HOUSE RFS

START
GR 852028

NEWTON
HOUSE
PLANTATION

WHITESTONE RIDGE

ROBIN HOODS BAY ROAD

GOATHLAND

PICKERING

YORK CROSS RFS

WIDOW HOWE
MOOR

FOSTER HOWES RFS

BLEA HILL RISE

STONEY
LEAS

FYLINGDALES
RADAR
(M.O.D.
PROPERTY)

## 18. NEWTON HOUSE PLANTATION AND LITTLEBECK
### (Ruswarp/Sleights option)

Map          – OS 27

Start point  – GR852028 – Carpark area on Goathland approach road from A169 (heading south from Whitby).

Distance     – Via Littlebeck approximately 11 miles (6 miles off road/5 miles on road). Taking Ruswarp/ Sleights extension – approximately 16 miles (6 miles off road/10 miles on road).

Time         – Approximately 3 hours – short ride/4 hours – long ride.

GOAW factor – 1.5 – 2.

**Introduction:**
A very rideable route if you do not like too much walking. Early summer is probably the best time to tackle this one in order to avoid the worst of the wet weather and the bracken. It is an interesting ride which takes you behind the Fylingdales Early Warning Radar Station and then turns away towards the coast. Travelling on fairly well-used tracks in a not too exposed environment should be enjoyable for the rider who is not feeling too energetic and who wants the

option of extending the ride in the later stages if they feel like going a little further. Both long and short options include a steep climb at the end, but you are back at the start shortly after.

**The route:**

Start from the carpark area at the crossroads situated around 0.33 miles after leaving the A169. Head south-east on the track back towards the A169, crossing the road and accessing the moor via the gateway. Follow the bridleway downhill in the same south-easterly direction, with Newton House Plantation on your left-hand side for about 1.5 miles until you reach the junction at York Cross Rigg – here you should take the right-hand track.

From here the track climbs gently up Foster Howes Rigg. You will have to ride to the left-hand side of the perimeter fence which encloses the Fylingdales Early Warning Radar Station. The bridleway is not very well-used, and is pretty damp in places which could make this a difficult ride in winter conditions. Keep riding to the crossroads just before Stony Leas, and go through the gate on your right. Ride around the trig point and cairn to a 4-way marker post just beyond.

At the marker post, turn left on the Robin Hoods Bay path, which is actually a bridleway. Head in a north-easterly direction, keeping a couple of hundred metres from Blea Hill Beck and the edge of the plantation. The first part of the track is a stony downhill section, making for technical riding in any weather. Further along, in summer, the track is very over-grown by heather and bracken, and splits several times as you try to navigate the clearest way through – making things even more difficult. At some points you can be shoulder deep in bracken, and can lose sight of your tyres as the heather encroaches onto the track – so be careful of some of the deeper ruts and boggy areas which you encounter on the way, and which can easily send you over the handlebars if you sink your front wheel far enough in a boggy bit.

After approx. 2 miles you approach Shooting House Rigg, at GR901019. Here the track veers in a north-easterly direction and heads towards the junction of the Scarborough-Whitby road (A171) with the Ruswarp road (B1416). This is your eventual goal and you should reach it after some 1.25 miles. At places this track virtually disappears, but follow it as best you can north-east, east and then north-east again from the beck to the road. If you do lose the track, get off and walk as it's easier than trying to ride through heather, and less damaging.

Head west now on the B1416 Ruswarp road for around 1.5 miles, until you reach the junction for May Beck, Newton House and Littlebeck. Here you have to choose whether to take the shorter route, by descending the steep hill in front of you into Littlebeck, or to continue on the road to Ruswarp and Eskdale.

If you go down into Littlebeck, cross the stream in the village and begin the climb up past Hilltop Farm. A couple of hundred metres after the farm, the road turns right and a track continues directly ahead of you up the hill. Take this track uphill. After going through a gate onto the moor, veer right up the hillside and head towards the A169 as it crosses Sleights Moor, heading for Whitby. When you arrive at the road, turn left and climb up the hill back to your start point, which is the second junction on the right.

If you take the longer option you have an easy descent over 2 miles on the B1416 to Ruswarp. When you arrive in the village, you cross the River Esk, turn left and head for Sleights along the course of the river. After 1.25 miles you arrive in Sleights where you turn left onto the A169. Climb up through the village and begin the steep climb up Blue Bank onto the Pickering road. The road continues to climb, gradually easing as you reach the highest parts of Sleights Moor. Approx. 2.25 miles after leaving Sleights, you arrive back at the start point.

Whichever of the two options you choose, both have very steep climbs, but the Littlebeck route is the shorter climb of the two.

Fylingdales Moor from Whinstone Ridge

Windmill, Ravenscar. *Photo: Paul Hannon*

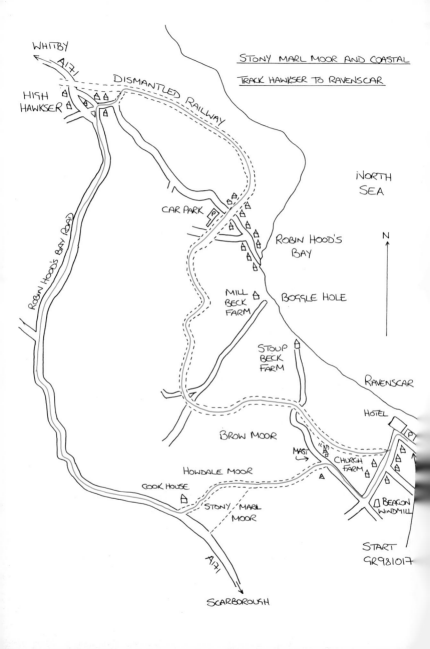

STONY MARL MOOR AND COASTAL
TRACK HAWKSER TO RAVENSCAR

WHITBY
A171

HIGH
HAWKSER

DISMANTLED RAILWAY

ROBIN HOOD'S BAY (ROAD)

CAR PARK

NORTH
SEA

N

ROBIN HOOD'S
BAY

MILL
BECK
FARM

BOGGLE HOLE

STOUP
BECK
FARM

RAVENSCAR

HOTEL

BROW MOOR

MAST

CHURCH
FARM

HOWDALE MOOR

COOK HOUSE

STONY MARL
MOOR

BEACON
WINDMILL

START
GR981017

A171

SCARBOROUGH

## 19. STONY MARL MOOR AND COASTAL TRACK HAWSKER TO RAVENSCAR

Map            – OS 27

Start point    – GR981017 – Carpark in Ravenscar.

Distance       – 18 miles (8 miles off road/10 miles on road).

Time           – Approximately 2 – 2.5 hours.

GOAW factor – 1.

**Introduction:**
This is the only route which follows a coastal track, mainly because access for cyclists along the coast is very restricted. You therefore need to look after this one to ensure that access, currently granted on a permissive basis by the council, is maintained and not jeopardised by any unthinking behaviour likely to cause complaints from landowners or walkers. Save this ride for a sunny day and take a picnic with you as there are some great spots on the sea cliffs to sit down and get a sun tan whilst enjoying the views over Robin Hood's Bay. If you have not visited the brilliant little coastal village of Robin Hood's Bay previously, you must pause for a look around its tiny lanes and streets and imagine several generations of fishermen and smugglers eking out a living in this isolated spot. There are a few tearooms, a couple of pubs

and plenty of shops catering to the day-trippers, although you might find a few of these closed if you visit out of season. We would recommend a weekday or a Saturday in summer for this one, as you will probably find the place swamped on Sundays. There is no real hard work on the route, and navigation is very easy.

**The route:**
Beginning at the carpark near the Ravenscar Hotel, ride uphill directly away from the sea and the hotel entrance. Continue straight on over the old railway line and past some buildings. You will see the remains of Beacon Windmill next to a house at the road junction some 0.75 miles from your start point. Turn right here, heading north-west along Scarborough Road towards the mast that you will see directly ahead of you on the hilltop.

On reaching the mast you will see a bridleway sign on the left, signposted to Hellwath. Follow this downhill over Stony Marl Moor, taking the right-hand fork (blue arrow for bridleway) when the track divides. This leads you downhill and soon joins the farm access road leading to Cook House. Here you turn left, past the farm entrance, and climb the short rise to reach the main Scarborough to Whitby road. This part of the route is around 3.3 miles in distance.

Turn right onto the main road, the A171. Follow this road for just over 3 miles. At the fork at Sneaton Corner take the right fork, continuing on the A171, or what is now called Robin Hood's Bay Road. The road now climbs very gently and then starts to descend. About 1.5 miles on from the fork you reach the hamlet of Normanby. Here the descent continues, carrying you all the way down to High Hawsker. The village is signposted at a steep fork off to your right some 6.24 miles after joining the main road. Be careful about crossing the road to enter High Hawsker, as the traffic comes down the road behind you very fast and you do not want to be sat in the middle of this road waiting to cross. As a general caution this is probably the busiest road used in the whole guide and care is needed about the traffic overtaking you on the narrower downhill stretches – make sure you stick to the edge and are highly visible to overtaking traffic.

It should only take around 30 minutes to get the road section finished, and then the best bit begins. Riding into High Hawsker, turn right at the junction signposted to Robin Hood's Bay and climb up the hill out of the village. At the top of the hill the road turns right and you will see a caravan park sign directly ahead of you and a lane leading directly towards the sea. Walk down this short lane (designated a footpath), past the caravan site, for the hundred yards or so until you reach the disused railway line crossing the lane from left to right. You follow this to the right.

The lane is a cinder track with a fairly good surface and leads you along the coast. Follow it around, travelling parallel to the coastline with beautiful sea views. After some 2 miles you cross over the spring which feeds the waterfalls at Rain Dale. The track now begins to swing round to the right, arriving eventually in Robin Hood's Bay. Here you leave the track, cross the road which leads down the hill into the bay, and ride into the carpark opposite. At the bottom of the carpark there is a lane downhill for a hundred yards or so, and then you join another road, turning right, and the railway line recommences a hundred yards on your left.

Follow the track south-west out of Robin Hood's Bay. After crossing the road from Robin Hood's Bay to Fylingthorpe the track heads due south as you follow it over Middlewood Lane then crossing Ramsdale Beck. After travelling south for about 2 miles the track enters Allison Head Wood. Follow the track through the wood, over two clearings as it swings towards the east. The track now follows the contours of Brow Moor, which you crossed at the onset of the route. This section again opens up to provide sea views and there are a few excellent spots to sit and have a bite to eat whilst taking in the views.

Continue travelling east, crossing over Scarborough Road. Approx. 2 miles after leaving the wooded area you arrive back in Ravenscar where you turn left on the road to return to the start point.

**It should be mentioned that the former railway line is not a public right of way, but is a permissive right of way by courtesy of Scarborough Borough Council and both cyclists and walkers enjoy access currently. You will almost definitely encounter walkers on this track and should be careful on the narrower sections and always pass them at their pace.**

Overlooking Robin Hood's Bay from the coastal track

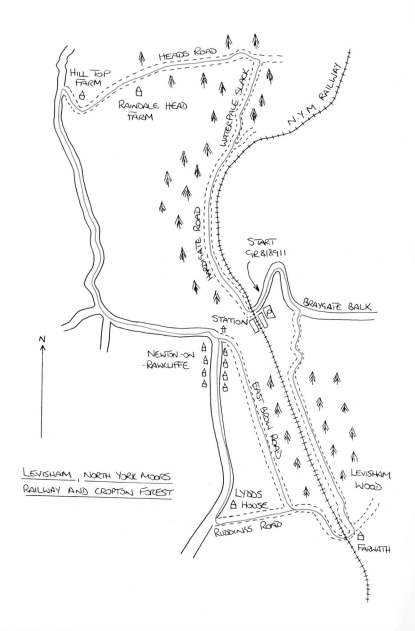

HEADS ROAD

HILL TOP FARM

RAINDALE HEAD FARM

WATERPALE SLACK

N.Y.M. RAILWAY

HARDGATE ROAD

START GR 818911

BRAYGATE BALK

STATION

NEWTON-ON-RAWCLIFFE

EAST BROW ROAD

LEVISHAM, NORTH YORK MOORS RAILWAY AND CROPTON FOREST

LEVISHAM WOOD

LYNDS HOUSE

RUDDINGS ROAD

FARWATH

N

## 20. LEVISHAM, NORTH YORK MOORS RAILWAY AND CROPTON FOREST

Map           – OS 27

Start point   – GR818911 – Levisham Station.

Distance      – 13 miles (9-11 miles off road/2-4 miles on road,
                depending on route chosen).

Time          – Approximately 2.5 – 3 hours.

GOAW factor – 1.

**Introduction:**
Definitely a dry weather ride, so leave this one until after a sustained period of dry weather (if such a thing ever happens!) as the section along the railway line on the return section can get very boggy at the best of times. Care needs to be taken with the navigation at the beginning of this ride, but once past Heads Road it is very easy to follow the ride. We would personally advocate the road option from Newton-on-Rawcliffe down to Ruddings Road as being a more pleasant one to ride, with not much traffic about. Also, you do not want to be too close to the sewage works in dry, hot weather!

**The route:**

Starting from the railway station, cross the line with care and turn to the right to follow the forest track, Hardigate Road, which heads due north, parallel to the railway line. **This section of track is a permissive path. Please cycle with care and give way to all pedestrians and other users.** After around 1.4 miles you will see a stream crossing under the track. Straight after this is a marker post on your left-hand side which indicates a track climbing to the left.

Take this track which begins to climb around to the right. It leads you up onto the hillside with views to your right towards Levisham Moor, where you will see the ruins of Skelton Tower on Corn Hill Point.

After a few more yards on the main track you pass a single tree on your left-hand side, with a marker post just beyond it. Take the track off to the left, climbing steeply around to the right, and head up to Waterpale Slack. Once onto more level ground, you will see another marker post. Keep left – more or less straight on – at this stage and follow the track through the forest for another few hundred yards. Eventually you reach the forestry road, Heads Road, which forms a T-junction with the track you are following.

Turn left onto Heads Road and follow this level road along Raindale Head. Soon the road swings sharp right out onto a clearing and you pass Hill Top Farm – approximately 4 miles from your start point. Descend the hill past the farm to join Stape Road heading due south. Turn left and follow the road as it climbs a little, before descending for around a mile. Soon after passing Rawcliffe House Farm on your right you arrive at a T-junction near a campsite. Turn left here and continue into Newton-on-Rawcliffe. On entering the village you have a choice of route: either to turn left and follow the lane along

122

Levisham Bottoms from Braygate Balk

Careful crossing the tracks at Levisham!

the top of Newton Banks and East Brow Banks; or to follow the road through Newton, descending past Lydds House.

If you choose the back lane past Newton, you enjoy a great view down over your start point in the valley – but then have to pass the site of a sewage works further on, as well as a farm scrapyard which is none too scenic. Whichever route you choose you will eventually arrive at a junction with Ruddings Road – at GR812886 (village route) or GR823887 (scenic? route). You will then turn left and head due east towards Farwath Road.

Descend this steep track through the woods to reach the railway line again. Cross the stream either by the footbridge, or by the ford. Cross the railway line and take the wooden footbridge alongside the railway line which leads to a gate on your right. Go through the gate into the field and head to your left to follow the bridleway below the woods, heading due north through Levisham Wood.

Follow the track through the woods, keeping parallel to the railway line, and heading for Keldgate Slack. After approx. 1.25 miles you reach the outcrop. Follow the track below it and around it, then climb up the hill straight ahead to rejoin the road from Levisham. Turn left onto the road and enjoy the descent over the last few hundred yards down to your start point. The descent is steep at first but eases out as the road doubles back on itself round to the left.

The track through the wood can be very muddy in winter conditions, and you should be prepared to walk this part at this time of year.

The narrow streets of
Robin Hood's Bay

Gary McLeod

## MOUNTAIN BIKE ORGANISATIONS/CLUBS

The British Mountain Bike Federation
36 Rockingham Road
Kettering
Northants. NN16 8HG
Telephone 0536 412211

The British Mountain Bike Federation is the National Govern-
ing body for the sport and pastime of mountain biking, and is
recognised as such by the Sports Council, other cycling
bodies, and by other statutory bodies such as the Countryside
Commission and the Forestry Commission. It was formed in
1990 on the initiative of a number of people who all felt there
was a need for a national body which would cater for the
needs of mountain bikers.

The BMBF is a non profit-making organisation which aims
for increased acceptance of the sport, and increased aware-
ness of the needs of mountain bikers in the countryside. Their
plans revolve around development of mountain biking for
sport, recreation and conservation.

Membership of the BMBF is priced extremely keenly, and
gives members the benefit of world-wide third party insurance cover, free legal advice, access to internationally
recognised racing licences, newsletters, preferential rate
insurance and discounts on gear and clothing. Full details
from the BMBF membership secretary.

**Local Clubs:**

Cleveland Mountain Bike Club    Mr R Barnard
83 Park Lane
Guisborough
Cleveland   TS14 6PA

Leeds Mountain Bike Club    Mr P Morphet
27 St. Michaels Road
Headingley
Leeds   LS6 3BG

Jorvik Mountain Bike Club    Mr K. Neale
61 Millfield Road
Scarcroft Road
York

North of England Mountain
Bike Association (N.E.M.B.A.)    Secretary
68 Heidelberg Road
Heaton
Bradford
West Yorkshire   BD9 5EB

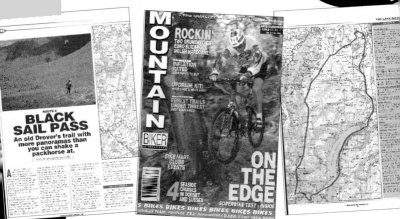

# Get off-road every month with MBi

# THE BEST TRAILS IN BRITAIN

For day trips, weekends or week holida

* Marked clearly on OS maps

* All local information
  Accommodation, approach routes,
  and supplies

* Backcopies of MBi are available
  Please order via the magazine

* 1993's routes include;

  West Yorkshire, Scotland coast to coast,
  Shropshire, the French Riviera, Kielder, Isle
  of Man, Lake District, the North York Moors,
  the Cotswolds, the Quantocks, mid-Wales, t
  North Pennines, Wharfedale, Exmoor, the Pe
  District, the Gower Peninsula and more.

* £2 at the newsagents

**MOUNTAIN BIKER INTERNATIONAL**